CONCILIUM

THEOLOGY IN THE AGE OF RENEWAL

CONCILIUM

CONCILIUM/VOL. 28

CANON LAW

POSTCONCILIAR THOUGHTS

RENEWAL AND REFORM OF CANON LAW

edited by ✠NEOPHYTOS EDELBY
TEODORO JIMÉNEZ URRESTI
PETRUS HUIZING, S.J.

Volume 28

CONCILIUM
theology in the age of renewal

PAULIST PRESS
NEW YORK, N.Y./GLEN ROCK, N.J.

NIHIL OBSTAT: John E. Brooks, S.J., S.T.D.
Censor Deputatus

IMPRIMATUR: ✠ Bernard J. Flanagan, D.D.
Bishop of Worcester

September 20, 1967

The Nihil Obstat and Imprimatur are official declarations that a book or pamphlet is free of doctrinal or moral error. No implication is contained therein that those who have granted the Nihil Obstat and Imprimatur agree with the contents, opinions or statements expressed.

Library of Congress Catalogue Card Number: 67-30868

Suggested Decimal Classification: 291.8

Paulist Press assumes responsibility for the accuracy of the English translations in this Volume.

PAULIST PRESS
EXECUTIVE OFFICES: 304 W. 58th Street, New York, N.Y. and 21 Harristown Road, Glen Rock, N.J.
Executive Publisher: John A. Carr, C.S.P.
Executive Manager: Alvin A. Illig, C.S.P.
Asst. Executive Manager: Thomas E. Comber, C.S.P.

EDITORIAL OFFICES: 304 W. 58th Street, New York, N.Y.
Editor: Kevin A. Lynch, C.S.P.
Managing Editor: Urban P. Intondi

Printed and bound in the United States of America by
The Colonial Press Inc., Clinton, Mass.

CONTENTS

PREFACE

✠Neophytos Edelby/*Damascus, Syria*

Teodoro Jiménez-Urresti/*Bilbao, Spain*

Petrus Huizing, S.J./*Louvain, Belgium*

The three years of preparation for Vatican Council II and its four sessions have been a time of basic re-thinking, in which more than a few doctrinal formulations on the Church, its human structures, mode of existence and ecclesiastical laws have been subject to revision and reform.

This task has been carried out with such intensity that Pope Paul VI, in the public session of November 18, 1965, could speak of a "new mentality", a "new consciousness", at work in the Church. This consciousness, embracing as it does a striving for greater purity and depth of Christian life, a more authentic witness, affects not only the members of the Christian Churches, but also their ecclesiastical structures and laws. It is a deeply important outcome of the Council and has stamped the whole Church as having what might be termed a "post-conciliar mentality".

This mentality and consciousness are bound to produce canonical renewal and reform. The Council decrees themselves have fixed its bases and guiding lines. And in the two years that have elapsed since the Council itself, legislation has already been initiated as a first step toward the new Code of Canon Law outlined by the Council.

All this has contributed to a deeper understanding of the Church as an historical reality. But it has also produced, by way of counterpart, such an atmosphere of precariousness and rela-

1

tivity where still extant pre-conciliar legislation is concerned that it has sometimes led to anarchical attitudes and expressions. These, in their anxiety to adopt a conciliar tone, would treat the pre-conciliar code as already outdated.

This note of precariousness is intensified if one remembers that much of the pre-conciliar legislation still in force is actually centuries old, since although the Code itself only came into operation fifty years ago (in 1918), it codified, improving on technicality of expression, legislation which had originated and been formulated long before—quite apart from the fact that the world has moved forward a whole age from half a century ago.

This volume of *Concilium* partakes of this historical background and shares in this post-conciliar atmosphere with the intention of putting forward some reflections that will help toward a clearer understanding of the gravity and seriousness with which canonical decisions must be taken on some basic points.

First of all, while remembering that the Church is constituted and organized in this world as a society (*Constitution on the Church,* n. 8), it must not be forgotten that its ecclesiastical structure and what comes under its dominion must spring from the very heart of the basic social structure given by Christ himself, and that a theology must therefore remain intact, through being intangible, in Canon Law (Echevarría). Yet theologians and canonists must always remember that the elaboration of Canon Law is not the same thing as creating theology (Jiménez-Urresti).

Once these basic points are established, it is particularly interesting, in view of the future Code of Canon Law, to examine the advantages and disadvantages that a canonical codification can have in the life of the Church (Huizing), and to have a clear view on whether it is worth establishing a common Code for the whole Church, or whether a number of different codifications might not be a better historical solution for the Church, which is, after all, a "body of Churches" (*Constitution on the Church,* n. 23) each with its own characteristics, history and individual peculiarities (Edelby).

The experiences gained from a fifty-year-old Code enables us to reflect with mature judgment on the prospect of another codification (Shannon); and the attempts made by a group of canonists from a world fully launched into the new age deserve particular attention (Boyle). Any codification, including that of Canon Law, must begin by formulating the principles or bases of a constitutional Canon Law (Heimerl).

These general considerations lead to an examination of two states (hierarchy and religious) which determine the constitutional canonical functioning of the Church, as shown at particular levels of this constitutional functioning: bishops in episcopal conferences (Munier), and religious in diocesan pastoral work (Proesmans).

Professor John Oesterreicher contributes a consideration of Vatican Council II's *Declaration on the Jews,* taking into account the reactions of Jewish writers.

Since positive Canon Law belongs to the human and historical side of the Church, and to the social part of that side, that is, to the most external part, it should not be surprising to state that Canon Law, as perhaps no other positive aspect of the Church can, reflects the pilgrim, historical, contingent and changing aspect that the Church possesses in the midst of its unchanging condition. Canon Law is continually reminding the Church that it is immersed in the world, time and space, and so undergoes the pressures and limitations natural to these factors (*Constitution on the Church,* n. 8). It even reminds the Church that it is weak and needs the comfort of the power of God's grace if it is not to waver from perfect fidelity (n. 9), that its holiness is imperfect (n. 48), since it embraces sinners, and is in need of constant and perpetual reform. This is why Canon Law cannot do without the penal side that is natural to it.

The Bibliographical Survey examines the contributions of canonists to this penal Canon Law (Huizing) and on its adaptation to the times and local conditions in the Eastern Churches (Žužek).

To sum up, for the Church to enter into the history of mankind (*Constitution on the Church*, n. 9) and be a social reality of history (*Constitution on the Church in the Modern World*, n. 44), with all the consequences of this, but at the same time remaining true to its institutions, which pertain to the present time, it must take on the appearance of this passing time (*Constitution on the Church*, n. 48).

PART I
ARTICLES

Lamberto de Echevarría / *Salamanca, Spain*

The Theology of Canon Law

"It is possible to talk of a theology *of* Canon Law *in* Canon Law", it was stated in the Introduction to the first *Canon Law* volume of *Concilium*. This echoes the declaration made in the encyclical *Mystici Corporis*: "Canon Law and theology are united by close ties." Canon Law does in fact start from pre-juridic bases and has a meta-juridic end, both of these provided by theology. So it is opportune to try to clarify the relationship between canonical ordering and theological data by reflecting on the suggestions made in the spate of literature currently appearing on the subject, evidence in itself of its particular relevance.

I

THE TRADITIONAL EXPOSITION

In the 19th century, ecclesiology produced a system which for convenience we can call "traditional", even in the knowledge that the same expression can be applied to much earlier and more interesting systems. It was centered on a juridical idea, of the "perfect society", and reasoned thus: (1) Christ desired a perfect society. which (2) requires a juridical ordering similar (3) to that of the State. This was a sort of "juridical sociology", built

7

up of elements whose origin was theological. It would be interesting to compare a juridical dictum on the nature of a corporation with texts of 19th-century ecclesiology: ignoring the fact that one would be using the legal code of the country or some international treaty as its authority and the other, sacred scripture, their construction would be identical.

A result of this approach is that the reality of the Church is seen as something that can be clearly perceived, not as essentially a mystery. There is an undisguised attempt to copy civil law and the technique is the same, that of jurisprudence in general terms and in particular that of codification. The effect is a Code of Canon Law based on a plan common to several civil codes, pagan in origin, in which, for example, sacraments are treated as "things" and the division of parishes becomes a matter of Property Law.

II

CRITICISMS OF THIS SYSTEM

The value of this system is becoming more and more questionable as attacks on it multiply. One factor in these attacks has been increased contact between Catholics and Orthodox, particularly as a result of the Russian diaspora following the 1917 Revolution, and as a consequence of a general improvement in communications. Catholics have learned from this that the Orthodox accuse them of having "naturalized, secularized, materialized and paganized the idea of a Church".[1] There have also been closer contacts with Protestantism, and there, Catholics find the idea of an invisible, purely spiritual Church, hostile to law. A whole, fascinating, new terminology is revealed to them.

The Protestant criticism of the traditional Catholic approach was summed up in Sohm's famous book *Kirchenrecht,* published in Leipzig in 1892, which made a deep impression. Modernism, with its stresses on charity (Harnack), purely moral bonds (Saba-

[1] Y. Congar, "Saint Eglise", in *Unam Sanctam* 41, (Paris, 1963), p. 207.

tier), and the charismatic structure (Buonaiutti), intensified the attack still further. Since 1940 it has been carried on by some writings of the Italian canonical school based on a cold positivism (the theory of "Ordering").[2]

All these questions posed the problem in no uncertain terms: the problem of whether Canon Law is theologically justifiable at all, and if so, how?

The reply had to come from the field of ecclesiology. But this discipline has in the last few years been undergoing some really spectacular changes (as Olivier Rousseau has demonstrated[3]), and also provided grounds for further attacks based on a false understanding of itself, such as those of Klein, originally from within and later more increasingly from outside the Catholic camp. These attacks have left their mark in a certain anti-juridical general climate (described by López Ortiz[4]) which was by no means alien to the Council itself.

When Vatican Council II finally produced its great document on the Church, canonical organization was not expressly mentioned in it, and its traditional prop, the notion of a perfect society, was systematically avoided. But when the *Constitution on the Church* is taken as a whole, it is clear that the Council has seen the instrumental importance of Canon Law—and puts forward the essential elements for its complete revision.

This deep change in traditional ecclesiology is disconcerting for the canonists, but it does offer a splendid opportunity for re-thinking the essential theological basis of Canon Law.

[2] "The bases and various enunciations (of the theory of order) are spoiled by failing to provide a coherent link with certain postulates of traditional philosophy": J. Hervada, "El concepto de ordenamiento canónico", in *Ius Canonicum* 5, (1965), p. 61.

[3] O. Rousseau, "The Constitution 'Lumen Gentium' in the context of the movements for the reform of theology and pastoral of the last decades", in Barauna (ed.), *L'Eglise de Vaticane II*, (Paris, 1966), Vol. II, pp. 35-56. (An English translation is being prepared by Franciscan Herald Press, Chicago.)

[4] Cf. J. López Ortiz in *Ius Canonicum* 6, (1966), pp. 5-24.

III

TOWARD A THEOLOGICAL CONSTRUCTION

Article 8 of the *Constitution on the Church* reveals the complexity of the basic idea of the Church:

> Christ, the one mediator, established and ceaselessly sustains here on earth his holy Church, the community of faith, hope and charity, as a visible body, through which he communicates truth and grace to all. But the society structured with hierarchical organs and the mystical body of Christ are not to be considered as two realities, nor are the visible assembly and the spiritual community, nor the earthly Church and the Church enriched with heavenly things; rather they form one complex reality which combines a divine and a human element.

The result is an organism subject, by its very nature, to a series of tensions. It is a holy Church, and made up of sinners; it carries within itself a hierarchical structure of authority, and at the same time claims the charisms as naturally belonging to it; it is in the world, yet has—and in a certain way anticipates here on earth—an eschatological end; it is juridically ordered, and yet its true bond of unity is communion in charity.

Following Pius XII in *Mystici Corporis* and Paul VI in his address of November 20, 1965, the Council rejected the contradiction supposed to exist between the *"Liebeskirche"* and the *"Rechtskirche"*, the Church of love and the Church of law, in order to demonstrate that there is but one Church, the Church of Christ.

The Council described this Church as an institution: "the prolongation of Christ", in the graphic definition of some eminent ecclesiologists. And this institution, whatever exact import is given to the word,[5] embraces the *idea* of an order, a structure,

---

[5] Cf. the magnificent article by M. Bergmann, of Taizé, "L'Institution", in *Verbum Caro* 20, (1967), pp. 42-65.

an authority, as opposed to the mere existence of these things, which could merely be the casual result of some quality or interest in the Church. This is why Pope Paul VI said: "Being by the will of its founder a perfect social body, it must necessarily have a visible existence which means that it should be governed by laws."

From outside the Church it is clearly possible to quarrel with this institutional concept, which in ecumenical circles tends to be known as "Catholic", but obviously once it is admitted, it logically postulates the existence of a certain juridical order, the extent and characteristics of which leave room for further discussion. The Pope remarks that "this divine ordinance in no way conflicts with natural law; . . . but rather is eminently congruent to it".[6]

Modern ecclesiology, backed up with sound reasoning, has called the institution known as the Church a "radical sacrament" insofar as it is, in Bertrams' phrase, "the sacred symbol which both signifies and effects supernatural grace",[7] a concept which complements, not contradicts, that of the mystical body.[8] This "radical sacrament" in itself defines the outline of the juridical structure it carries with it. It is the very nature of the Church as a radical sacrament, going beyond the mere necessity of imposing a certain order on the multitude (which could be derived from a simple consideration of juridical philosophy, or from a parallel with the People of God marching through the desert), beyond the need to organize adequately the different functions proper to an organic body,[9] that leads us to consider canonical ordering in its substance and functioning.

The first thing that the Church as radical sacrament proposes

[6] This congruence has been fully studied by A.-M. Stickler, in his article on the mystery of the Church in Canon Law, in Hölbock and Sartory (eds.), El Misterio de la Iglesia, (Barcelona, 1966), Vol. II, pp. 127-224 and in particular pp. 129-39.

[7] W. Bertrams, "Die Eigennatur des Kirchenrechts", in Gregorianum 27, (1946), p. 564.

[8] M. Useros, "Statuta ecclesiae" y "Sacramenta ecclesiae" en la Eclesiología de Santo Tomás de Aquino, (Rome, 1962), p. 167, n.49.

[9] Cf. the article by A. de la Huerga on the Church of love and the Church of law, in La Potestad de la Iglesia, (Barcelona, 1960), pp. 25-9.

for our consideration is an activity of a cultual nature, based on the order of charity and oriented primarily toward God. The discipline of this activity supposes: (1) the juridical safeguarding of the Word of God, which is received, kept and spread by the Church; (2) the sacraments, and particularly the eucharist, with the norms governing its celebration. (In this way the Thomist conception of the Church acting *per fidem et fidei sacramenta* is put into effect.)

It also offers an activity of a functional type, insofar as the Church faces the world that surrounds it as a sign, concerned with the evangelization of this world. This supposes that its structures are adequately ordered to pastoral needs and missionary requirements. So it must be concerned with: (1) its ministers organized into pastoral functions (universal, diocesan or parochial); (2) the different states of its faithful (religious and lay); (3) making rules and where necessary correcting its faithful through penances; and, finally (4) glorifying the faithful after their death.[10] All these institutions must be imbued, of course, with a genuinely evangelical spirit, so that by their simplicity, their sense of continuity with what their divine founder stood for in this world, they will be an effective witness to the New Law, and never a contradiction of it.

This supposes that the Church will possess a *power* received from its divine founder, a power that will in a sense be a prolongation of the power that was his.[11] The Council has deliberately defined this power as *sacramental* in origin and as *serving* in character. This it does whenever it refers to it and particularly when it talks of the episcopate. However, this serving characteristic can be overemphasized, which is why Pope Paul VI, in his address, insisted that the note of genuine "authority" must always be preserved. It is a notable achievement of the Council to have recognized, and to have stamped, to a certain extent, with the

[10] I am following the classification proposed by Useros in his (Latin) article on Canon Law in the life of the Church and its adaptation in the light of the New Law, in *Rev. Esp. Der. Can.* 18, (1963), pp. 659-65.

[11] Cf. A. de la Huerga and H. Heimerl, "Aspecto cristológico del Derecho canónico", in *Ius Canonicum* 6, (1966), pp. 25-51.

weight of its authority, the idea that this power in the Church forms one whole, as ecclesiologists were already beginning to see. Within this whole, for good technical reasons and out of respect for an ancient tradition, there is a distinction between "order" and "jurisdiction", but this distinction should not be exaggerated, as these are not two separate and independent powers, but two parts of a whole.

IV

ORDER IN THE CHURCH

The implementation of this power in the inner life of the Christian faithful tends to implant the order of grace by which they are united to their head, Jesus Christ, particularly through faith, baptism and the eucharist. But it also tends toward an appropriate external order that shows more in the right ordering of ecclesial activities, and the impetus toward this, than in resolving actual or potential juridical conflicts, which is rather the aim of civil order. Thus, order in the Church appears in the accessibility of the best means for the faithful to obtain the *salus animarum* which is the ultimate end of ecclesial activity.

This order in the Church is, however, the result of an extremely delicate adjustment of different postulates that are to some extent contradictory. For example, it has to reconcile unity with variety, as the Council has shown in its various documents, from the first to be approved, the *Constitution on the Sacred Liturgy,* to the more concrete dispositions made with regard to more specifically juridical aspects of Church life, as for example in the *Decree on the Pastoral Office of Bishops in the Church,* which established the requirements for episcopal conferences.[12] It also has the very difficult task of balancing right juridical order with the respect due to charisms, trying always to carry out the apostolic precept *spiritum nolite exstinguere,* while at the same time providing a

[12] Cf. the article by W. Stark on the routinization of charism as a characteristic of Catholicism, in *Sociological Analysis* 26, (1965), pp. 281-2.

channel and a norm for the prophetic function;[13] not to mention the equally difficult job of harmonizing tradition with the dynamic of renewal.

Therefore, this order in the Church is not something purely external, which would be pharisaism, but a spiritual order, rooted in the inmost depths of the souls of the faithful. This is why canonical order can never be purely juridical, but will always be broadly based on the moral order.

V

LAW AND PASTORAL CARE

The Council showed a clear preference for the pastoral side of Church activity, following in this the orientation given it by Pope John XXIII. Just as it avoided using the expression "the Church militant", so it always preferred to emphasize the "pastoral function" of those in positions of authority, rather than authority *tout court*. This same pastoral care made it anxious not only to ensure the efficacity of its dispositions, but also to attend to the proper liberty of its members, which must not be unduly repressed nor suffocated with an excess of precepts.

This is why it has been thought preferable to substitute the concept of "pastor" for the third element in the traditional description of the threefold office of Christ—Lord, priest and king —thereby avoiding all possibility of contrasting the power to rule or govern with that of instructing. Both elements go to make up one reality, and the rule of the Church is juridical and pastoral at the same time. This lesson from the Council is of utmost importance but does not seem to have been understood by all commentators.

What follows from this is an understanding of Law as an instrument, profoundly religious in content, not self-justifying in its activity, a technique to be employed in the service of the transcendent aims of the Church.

[13] Cf. the interesting ideas put forward by Ch. Journet, in ed. Barauna, *op. cit.*, II, pp. 299-312 (Fr. ed.).

VI

THE DYNAMIC OF THE CHURCH

Ecclesia semper reformanda, a Church in the constant throes of reform, is a concept generally recognized as one of the chief fruits of the ecclesiology of the Council. As Olivier Rousseau has written in the essay already cited: "The Constitution has tried to break with the static representation of the 'Church-entity' and bring out the dynamic character of the Church on the move, the new People of God, with sights fixed firmly on its eschatological end." The first aphorism could perhaps be complemented by another: *Ius canonicum semper reformandum,* to emphasize the need for a dynamic, questing Canon Law, in the constant throes of adaptation to the society in which the Church lives. It should, far from providing a target for the accusation of being "a theology of the *fait accompli*", be able to offer theology the vital material it needs if theological thought in the Church is to be able to carry out its functions fully and completely, and be able to do this because of its basis in uninterrupted contact with ecclesiastical reality.

It has not always been in a position to do this. Canon Law has at times been more of a drawback or obstacle to renewal in the Church. A failure to see what was not susceptible of reform in Canon Law, and what could be reformed, even though it might have a venerable tradition behind it, has led to a certain immobilism. If it was possible to reconcile this with the juridically-minded ecclesiology before the Council, there is absolutely no excuse for its continuation, after the Council has produced such a dynamic and lively account of the Church and of the place of Canon Law within the Church.

Teodoro Jiménez-Urresti/*Bilbao, Spain*

Canon Law and Theology: Two Different Sciences

The post-conciliar climate is becoming steadily more opposed to "juridicist theology". This touches on the natures of both theology and Canon Law. Some theologians would hold Canon Law to be a "theological science" or a "theological discipline", whereas many canonists would hold it to be a discipline of implementation. The argument can only be a sterile one as both sides define their terms differently, and can even be harmful if it is allowed to turn into a theological slanging match.

A useful analogy which might help to pacify both sides, both of which are in the right to a certain extent, could be the relationship between philosophy and law. There is a "philosophy of law", but the study of the law is not a philosophical discipline; it is the "legal science". Neither does the philosopher "do" law, though he studies the philosophy of the human phenomenon known as the law. The lawyer does not "do" philosophy but takes the principles he needs from it to apply them to his particular discipline. So the theologian does not "do" Canon Law, nor the canonist theology. There is a distinction and gradation in natural sciences, and in the sciences of faith, the ecclesial sciences.

17

I

THEOLOGICAL SCIENCE

The Church is an "event" as well as an "institution", divine and human, the community of faith, hope and charity as well as a society visibly constituted (*Constitution on the Church*, n. 8). The nature and relationship of these aspects of event and institution as instituted by Christ, studied "by the power of God's grace promised to her by the Lord", that is, according to revealed truth, is the business of the science of theology.

· The results of this theological study will form the basic data for the discipline of Canon Law. They are the "fundamental structures" of the Church (*Ecclesiam suam*, n. 41), which cannot be subject to reform but command faithful observance. Thus, Canon Law embraces a theology.

We also know—and it is the task of theology to make it known—that in the Church "the human is ordered to the divine", just as the social and visible is a sign and instrument of the invisible, of the life of the Church in the Trinity: the Church, as life-institution, is a "sacrament" by analogy with the mystery of the incarnate Word, its founder (*Constitution on the Church*, nn. 1, 8). This is its "basic conception" (*Ecclesiam suam*, n. 41). The structural-social side of the Church, therefore, is "sacramentary", in that it expresses the mystery (as far as it possibly can, "among shadows"), and orders itself to the mystery. This structure, which informs the whole of Canon Law, is a theological fact. It is all the theology *of* Canon Law. So there is a theology *of* Canon Law and a theology *in* Canon Law. Canon Law cannot exist, or is it conceivable, without a theology, and this theology is a part of ecclesiology.

II

THE SCIENCE OF CANON LAW

The canonist receives and assumes these theological data as *postulates* derived from another field and science superior to his own. And among them is one that he knows to be the principal and definitive one for him: the fact that Christ, when he founded the Church, ordained it as a society with social structures. These are not entirely fixed and unchanging in form, but there are certain primary bases, such as the hierarchical structure with its threefold ministry and social media or sacraments. Even these have ample scope for variety of expression and concrete application—the theologians talk of the "generic institution" of the seven sacraments and the hierarchy; that is, the canonist knows from theology that this "basic structure", this "substance" of *divine law* was instituted by Christ in general terms, leaving its particular forms and functioning to the decision of the hierarchy founded by him. For its historical application, this substance has to be given particular shape by the positive rulings of the hierarchy itself, by the rulings of ecclesiastical law.

And it is precisely the study of this ecclesiastical law, of this particularizing and ordering of the Church, that is the science proper to the canonist. Canon Law has rightly been called "the juridic mode of theologicity".

III

Two Sciences

Thus, Canon Law can be studied on two different levels: the theological, which studies the social aspect of the Church in its essence, in its transcendent inner value, its mystery; and the canonical, which studies its human, phenomenological, positive aspects.

Theology studies revealed data; its aim is to formulate revealed truth; it moves on a level appropriate to this truth, and defines it with doctrinal judgments. Canon Law, on the other hand, receives these theological data in generic form as they concern the basic social structure of the Church, and particularizes them in its laws. Its end is the good of the body politic of the Church; it moves on the level of the instrumental and positive, adapting its social instruments (laws) to its end and prescribing a social conduct with practical judgments, so that *canonical truth* consists in the fitting of its means to the end intended by the legislator—in their efficacity.

Theology can only give one doctrinal judgment, that of fittingness to the objective truth revealed, although it can formulate this in different languages and perspectives, and with differing degrees of profundity. But Canon Law can formulate as many judgments on as many concrete or particular aspects as the substance of the theological question and the prudence of the legislator permit. In other words: theology studies what is the will of Christ, while Canon Law prescribes how this will of Christ is to be fulfilled in the social-ecclesial field, that is, it studies the will of the Church, which has to be upheld within the will of Christ.

To take another aspect: theology can only give one type of judgment—doctrinal. Canon Law, on the other hand, being a science of detail and practice, does not have to confine itself to the same sort of language as theology, or use it with the same meaning. It can use another form of language, or the same in a different mold and with a different value (the practical value), since its object is to formulate instrumental practices ordained to a practical end, the social behavior which it aims to put forward. For example: it is not the same thing, theologically, to say that the hierarchy, when it grants ministerial licences to priests, gives them jurisdiction to hear confessions, as it is to say that it approves and does not annul the exercise of this jurisdiction which they received at their ordination. But Canon Law, which does not pretend to formulate theological doctrine, but to regulate conduct, can use either formula indiscriminately, since both, for practical purposes, define the same principle of the priest's behavior toward his constituted authority, i.e., his behavior within the hierarchical communion. In this, Canon Law is rather like mathematics: "The order of factors does not change the result."

From all this it follows that theology and Canon Law have different immediate ends, different fields of action; they operate on different levels, and can and do use a different language and logic. They are two different sciences, differentiated, above all, by the notes of instrumentality and particularization which play a part in Canon Law and not in theology.

IV

THE RELATIONSHIP BETWEEN THE THEOLOGIAN AND THE CANONIST

The foregoing leads to some important conclusions that can be summarized as follows:

1. The theologian should not forget that canonical judgments are never, in themselves and by themselves, theological judgments; he should not take canonical expressions as theological expressions or as theological argument. (The expressions may sometimes be the same, particularly in cases where a theological norm is not generic, but so particular in itself that it is canonically viable without needing to be made any more explicit by ecclesiastical law. This will not be learned from the canonical expression alone, but by comparing it with the theological law.) The theologian should take the canonical argument without its overtones of legal particularization, so as to extract the theological essence from it.

2. The canonist, on his part, although he knows that there is a theology at the heart of Canon Law, also knows that any social ordering has its own autonomy, its own rules, concepts and expressions, and that its various canons, articles and laws form their own system, orientated to the implementation of particular matters. In pursuing his own specific ends, he will have formed his own logical processes and system of reasoning and justification, but he will not propose these to the theologian.

3. But just as the theologian proposes data to the canonist, so the canonist proposes practical canonical results to the theologian. These, being the socialized concrete expressions of the divine law of the Church, are not only canonical facts but also theological facts, facts with a theological essence which must fit into the generic constitution of the divine law of the Church, and

so into theological doctrinal explanations and systematizations.

Thus, the task of Canon Law is to effect the actualization of generic divine law while being faithful to its theological basis, to make it function while being faithful to its inner sacramentary nature, and to order the ecclesial structure in fidelity to its transcendent aim of *salus animarum*. It can, however, be unfaithful to this threefold task. In this case, theology will tell it that this possible infidelity cannot be substantial, since the charisms of indefectibility and infallibility enjoyed by the Church apply to its substantive mission and so also to the practical functioning of its social structures, that is, to the practical conduct of Canon Law. And theology will deliver its judgments (of theological valuation) on whether Canon Law is being unfaithful or not, within the limits possible, in order to decide whether its reform is necessary. But theology must find a place and a justification in its doctrinal system for every canonical act considered legitimate, and so faithful to its theological roots, by Church authority (both magisterial and canonical), if it is not to appear insufficient. So the canonist, familiar as he is with the canonical relativity of the numerous and divergent legitimate disciplines offered by history, will help the theologian to take cognizance of the generic character of the theological principles underlying Canon Law, and so to open his theological horizons and not restrict them to the accidents of canonical acts.

If the theologian forgets this lesson, he will run the grave risk, into which some say theology has already fallen, of producing a "theology of *faits accomplis*", that is, simply to treat particular historical canonical acts as though they belonged to the category of theology, without stripping them first of their skin of canonical particularization to get at the theologian kernel they enclose. If he falls into this trap, the theologian will strangle Canon Law with the absolute tie of theological truth which he attributes to the surface of Canon Law.

As this crime already seems to have been committed more than once, it is not surprising that one hears the expression "de-theologizing" Canon Law, not in the sense of depriving it of its theological kernel, but of extracting this kernel without extraneous pieces hanging on. Furthermore, the theologian who is guilty of this crime is restricting the breadth which theological principles, by their generic nature, should possess, by identifying the principle with one of its possible particular applications. This is "juridicizing" theology, and is the reason for current demands for the "de-juridicizing of theology, for the replacement of "juridicist theology".

In other cases theology fails to shed sufficient light on theological principles which will form the basis for subsequent canonical decisions. Then Canon Law will defend itself as best it can, trying not to compromise doctrinal principles and generally holding back, which means that it will not be able to reflect the visage of the Church with the clarity desirable. But this would hardly be the fault of Canon Law.

V

Particular Difficulties

There is a particular difficulty involved in trying to confine the two disciplines to their proper spheres: that the Church moves in both at the same time. It exercises a doctrinal magisterium and so moves in the sphere of theology, and at the same time, being a visible society, possesses and effects a social order, and so moves in the sphere of implementation. But as the Church is not practicing a scientific discipline as such and is not too careful about confining its expression to terminology proper to one particular science or another, it often carries the same terminology over from one sphere to the other. So there is a sort of symbiosis in the life of the Church between one science and the other.

This involves the theologians in a fair amount of work and not a few delicate problems, and leaves the canonists somewhat chagrined. It means that the first task of both is to determine by their use of terms which science and logic are being used by the authority of the Church in any given pronouncement, since they will often find that the authority is exercising its doctrinal magisterium in canonical terms and establishing laws in theological terms. Vatican Council II spotted the difficulty; hence its efforts always to express the theology of the Church in strictly theological terms —not always completely successful.

On the other hand, the Church, a supernatural society, a "sacrament" and a "mystery", is also a society in a sense analogous to civil society, and so its "canon" law is "law" in a sense analogous to that of civil law. This is why Canon Law finds its roots, nature and end in theology, not in civil law, a fact which has sometimes in practice been overlooked. This is why many theologians and canonists are now rightly demanding a return of Canon Law to theology, a greater "theologizing" of Canon Law.

This is not to deny its relationship with civil law. Since it is a science on its own, and an autonomous one, being a science of implementation, it shares this with civil law, from which it can learn much in its autonomous aspect, i.e., in its work of particularization. This means that maintaining it in the proper relationship to both theology and civil law is one more task for, and source of tension between, theologians and canonists. That canonists have realized this is shown by the abundant literature of recent years dealing with the particular, "juridic" nature of canonical order, different in essence from civil order though coinciding with it in many of its forms. A guide to some of this literature will be found in the bibliography which follows.

BIBLIOGRAPHY

1. *Canon Law in General*

Edelby, Jiménez-Urresti, Huizing, "Canon Law and Theology", in *Concilium* 8 (Oct. 1965), pp. 3-6.
Bidagor, "De nexu inter theologiam et jus canonicum ad mentem F. Suárez", in *Gregorianum* 28 (1947), pp. 457-70. *Idem*, "El Espíritu del Derecho Canónico", in *Rev. Esp. Der. Can.* 13 (1958), pp. 5-30. (Trans. into Italian in *Ephem. Juris. Can.* and German in *Oester. Archiv. Kirchenr.*).
G. Renard, "Contributo allo studio dei rapporti tra Diritto e Teologia:

Positione del Diritto Canonico", in *Riv. Int. Filos. Dir.* 16 (1936), pp. 478-521.

K. Moersdorf, "Zur Grundlegung des Rechtes der Kirche", in *Mün. Theol. Zeitschrf.* 3 (1952), pp. 329-48.

J. Salaverri, "El Derecho en el misterio de la Iglesia", in *Rev. Esp. Theol.* (1954), pp. 207-73. *Idem,* in *Investigación y Elaboración del Derecho Canónico* (proceedings of the 5th Week of Canon Law, Barcelona, 1956), pp. 1-54. *Idem,* "Lo humano y lo divino en la Iglesia", in *XII Semana Teol.* Madrid, 1953), pp. 327-62.

M. Useros, "*Statuta Ecclesiae*" y "*Sacramenta Ecclesiae*" *en la eclesiología de Sto Tomas de Aquino.* (Sub-titled: A Thomist Reflection on the Law of the Church in parallel to the Present Ecclesiological-Canonical Debate, Rome, 1962.)

V. de Reina, "Eclesiología y Derecho Canónico; Notas metodológicas", in *Rev. Esp. Der. Can.* 19 (1964), pp. 341-66.

C. Kemmeren, *Ecclesia et Jus,* (Rome, 1963).

J. M. Ribas Bracons, "El Derecho divino en el ordenamiento canónico", in *Rev. Esp. Der. Can.* 20 (1965), pp. 267-320.

H. Heimerl, "Die Diskussion um das Kirchenrecht", in *Theol. prakt. Quartalschrf.* 115 (1966), pp. 50-4.

G. May, "Enttheologisierung des Kirchenrechtes", in *Archiv. f. kath. Kirchenr.* (1965, no. 2), pp. 370-6.

T. Jiménez-Urresti, "Ciencia y teología del Derecho Canónico, o lógica jurídica y lógica teológica", in *Lumen* 8 (1959), pp. 140-55. *Idem,* "Problemática actual en el tema 'Iglesia-Derecho', I: Desteologización del Derecho Canónico y desjuridización de la teología", in *Iglesia y Derecho,* (Proceedings of the 10th Week of Canon Law, Salamanca, 1965), pp. 81-95.

G. Baldanza, "La costituzione 'De Ecclesia' ed alcune considerazione sullo spiritu che deve animare la riforma del Codice di Diritto Canonico", in *Ephem. Juris Can.* 21 (1965), n. 1-2.

G. Fransen, "Derecho Canónico y teología", in *Rev. Esp. Der. Can.* 20 (1965), pp. 37-45.

2. *The Particular Nature of Canon Law*

P. Fedele, *Discorso generale sull'ordinamento canonico,* (Padua, 1941) is the basic book on the subject, and has been followed by copious publications, of which there is a full Bibliography in:

J. de Salazar Abrisquieta, *Lo jurídico y lo moral en el Ordenamiento canónico,* (Vitoria, 1960), v. pp. xi-xxi. Reviewed by M. Arteche, "Observaciones sobre lo jurídico . . . .", in *Jus. Can.* 1 (1961, no. 1), pp. 467-78.

G Lesage, *La nature du droit canonique,* (Ottawa, 1960), reviewed by J. de Ayala, *ibid.,* in *Jus. Can.* 2 (1962, no. 2), pp. 595-632.

J. Hervada, "Fin y características del ordenamiento canónico", in *Jus. Can.* 2 (1962, no. 1), pp. 5-110. *Idem,* "El concepto del ordenamiento canónico en la doctrina contemporánea", in *Jus. Can.* 5 (1965, no. 1), pp. 5-61.

Various; *Investigación y elaboración del Derecho Canónico,* (Proceedings of the 5th Week of Canon Law, Barcelona, 1956), and in this in particular:

L. de Echevarría, "Características generales del ordenamiento canónico", (pp. 55-76).

G. Forchielli, "Caratteri comuni e differenziali nel Diritto Canonico", (pp. 77-98).

Petrus Huizing, S.J./*Louvain, Belgium*

The New Codification of the Church Order: Nature and Limits

When Pius X published his Letter *Arduum sane munus,* on March 19, 1904, he made the purpose of the codification of Canon Law "that all Church laws, up to the present time, shall be brought together into one clear and orderly whole, leaving out those that are abolished or antiquated and adjusting the rest, where necessary, to present circumstances". The purpose of this codification consisted, therefore, in the first place in collecting and putting into order the existing legislation which was badly organized and spread out over a multitude of sources. The adjustment to present circumstances was only a secondary aim. But when Pope John announced a new revision of Canon Law for the first time in his address to the cardinals on January 25, 1959, he made this "greatly desired and expected adjustment" (*auspicato e atteso aggiornamento*) the main purpose. This purpose was more clearly determined by Pope Paul in his address to the Commission for the Revision of Canon Law on November 20, 1965: "Canon law must be revised with wisdom: it must be adjusted to the new mentality which prevailed at Vatican Council II, a mentality that attaches great value to pastoral care and the new needs of the People of God."

1. *The Nature of a New Codification*

The composition of a new Code of Canon Law is therefore not

in the first place a codification of existing legislation, and still less of the existing codex. The purpose is not in the first place to compose a well-ordered whole of Canon Law which brings together the additions and modifications that have appeared since 1918, including those that were published during and after the Council. The first aim is to re-think the whole existing Church order in the new spirit that animated the Council and was clearly expressed there.

Gradually we have come to realize what this means. The first publications that followed Pope John's announcement demanded indeed some radical modifications in general but only mentioned a few concrete points that were not quite so radical. More recent studies, particularly those dealing with specific sections of Church order, show a far greater awareness of the significance and dimensions of this work. People begin even to realize that it is perhaps impossible to provide a complete codification of a totally revised Church order within the foreseeable future.

The Council, and the letters and decisions of Pope John and Pope Paul connected with this, have opened up basic perspectives that show a wholly new approach. But insofar as the concrete expression of the many aspects of the Church's life is concerned, this new approach is still in full fermentation. In very many fields it is still far from clear what this development will lead to. The tension between those that demand a minimum of changes and those that want to go to the farthest possible limits is too high to allow any binding norms as yet.

It is, of course, true, as the whole of history shows, that a period of breakthrough and renewal will always end up with a certain stabilization. But exactly where this new balance will be achieved, and when, nobody can as yet foresee.

2. *The Growing Developments at Every Level*

The development that is taking place at every level of the Church's life does not only affect the "domestic" life of the Church but also its relations with other Churches and religions as well as with the world at large. It must be admitted that, even where the most basic institutions of Church order are concerned, we still do not know what concrete shape these relations will take. To give a few examples: the episcopal college will remain the living and operative sign of the unity of the Church, in faith, community and preaching, and the pope will remain, also in the future, a similar sign of the same unity in the episcopal college. But how the relations between authority and autonomy, between the personal authority of the pope and the collegiality of pope, bishops, clergy and laity will take concrete shape after a few decades, cannot possibly be laid down yet in any clear norms. There is agreement that there must be a large measure of autonomy for the local Churches and particularly the episcopal conferences. But when we look at the actual concrete situation in which the episcopal conferences find themselves we can see that many are not at present able to deal properly with matters of Church order, and some have hardly the opportunity to meet; and that even in the best organized conferences this autonomy will cost the bishops much time and much labor, with the result that this work can have an important effect on the whole function of the bishop. Here again, it is impossible to foresee how exactly a clear and certainly a uniform arrangement for the whole Church can be achieved.

All the various religious groups within the Church—taking "religious" in the broad sense of the word—are in the full process of development. The problems of the relationship between central and local administration, between religious authority and the individual religious person, the problems of cooperation and merging, and many other problems are all still in a state of provisional experimentation, and sometimes they have not even reached that state yet. I heard accidentally that the Congregation for Religious is allowing a period of twelve years for these experiments with the promise of wide scope when it is felt necessary to deviate from general norms of Canon Law. Perhaps it is not very difficult to think out in theory perfect schemes for ecclesiastical procedures, but what would this achieve in practice? Where would we find the staff, numerous enough, able and having the leisure, to work out these procedures? We all know that the unity of the various Christian Churches will never come about by a simple abolition of those Churches that are not united with Rome and an equally simple continuation of the Catholic Church with all its existing structures. How, then, this unity must develop and what kind of structures will then come about is not clear to anybody. And we can go on with such questions, right up to the issue of ecclesiastical property and ecclesiastical finance.

And so it seems unreasonable to me to expect of any expert body that it can produce within the foreseeable future a ready-made Code of Canon Law that would embody the whole new Church order in the spirit of the Council in fixed and clear norms.

3. *A Constitution for the Universal Church?*

From the above-mentioned address of Pope Paul to the Commission for the Revision of Canon Law one might conclude that he was thinking primarily of a very general constitution for the universal Church (*lex* or *constitutio fundamentalis*) which would only formulate the most fundamental principles of Church order. Several prominent canonists support such a general constitution.[1] Further legislation would then be worked out either in a codex for the Latin Churches and one for the Eastern Churches or it would be left wholly to the local Churches, particularly to the episcopal conferences and the local ordinaries. Neumann mentions special Church orders for large regions of the Church, that is, for regions of a homogeneous culture, or with their own theological and canonical tradition, like the Eastern Churches, or Churches that have developed on their own since the 16th century. These would be a kind of legal framework to be set up by

[1] See the very interesting remarks of J. Neumann, "Erwägungen zur Revision des kirchlichen Gesetzbuches," in *Tübinger Theologische Quartalschrift* 146 (1966), pp. 301ff.; and also, K. Moersdorf, "Streiflichter zur Reform des kanonischen Rechts," in *Archiv für katholisches Kirchenrecht* 135 (1966), pp. 46ff.; J. McGrath, "Canon Law for the Church and the Churches," in *The Jurist* 26 (1966), pp. 457ff., where the author also announces an article on the structure and content of a universal code.

the Roman Curia together with the hierarchy of the respective regions or traditions, and this framework would guarantee a certain unity of Church order within the universal Church.

But even a very general constitution must have an open character. Even the principles of Church order allow of very varied concrete expressions, and are therefore in this sense also in a state of development. One will have to beware particularly of proposing whatever concrete structure as of "divine right" (*ius divinum*), that is, that it is an absolutely unchangeable structure also in its concrete expression. For this "divine right" cannot be contained in absolutely unchangeable forms. The mandate given by Christ to Peter and the Twelve is of "divine right". But this right has taken on very different forms in the course of history, and no one can foretell what kind of forms it can take on in the future. Today we can only say that at the moment it is expressed in the pope and the episcopal college. And even that should be properly understood. It does, for instance, not mean that the whole concrete apparatus of pope and bishops is totally and exclusively of divine right. The same warning holds for all other institutions that used to be called "of divine right". But with this basic proviso it should be possible to indicate some basic outlines of the Church's structure and organization and to pin down some principles of the Church's active presence in society that may remain valid for a considerable period.

4. *Provisional Regulations*

For all other sectors of Church order and at every level the only line to take is to abandon for the moment any attempt at drafting an all-embracing Code within a relatively short time. A transition period like ours is far more in need of provisions demanded all the time by concrete circumstances and without pretending to be definitive. Typical examples of these are the organization of the episcopal Synod for the universal Church, set up by Pope Paul on September 15, 1965, and the provisional norms laid down for the execution of the conciliar Decrees about religious life and the missions, published on August 6, 1966. Both measures explicitly foresee the possibility of further developments and the norms for the execution leave plenty of scope for experimentation. It is noteworthy that both these measures, as well as the new instruction about the Congregation for the Doctrine of Faith (the former "Holy Office") of December 7, 1965, are concerned with structures of Church order. Insofar as the norm for the personal life of members of the Church are concerned, the abolition of the Index as a Church law and the corresponding disciplinary sanctions (June 14, 1966), the abolition of the prohibition of cremation and its sanctions (July 5, 1964), the reduction of the rules for fasting and abstinence to a token rule (February 17, 1966)—all these measures point in the direction of a gradual emancipation of personal religious life from positive laws and sanctions. The Church begins to concentrate on Christian principles and a Christian attitude without making specific expressions of religious practice compulsory by law. Here, too, we have an important indication of how Church order is developing.

What we need at the moment are measures for those matters that urgently demand them. These measures should be able to deal with concrete actual needs and do not have to be technically perfect from the point of view of codification. It is also necessary now to create regular, effective and wholly open-minded communication between the higher and lower levels of administration and the people. The one-sided imposition from on high of norms that are not necessary, or at least not understood as necessary, and the taking of decisions from below that will commit a whole community or at least very many members against their will are both equally destructive for a community that wants to be honestly, healthily and genuinely one in Christ. Both extremes lead to constant, bitter and mutual provocation: unrealistic decisions from on high prompt opposite reactions and irresponsible initiatives from below, and too individualistic or exclusive experiments below inevitably provoke reactionary measures at the top.

5. *Coordination*

Unless concrete circumstances demand it directly and clearly, it would seem that at present the drafting of definite norms is not desirable and even impossible. This does not mean that the various administrative bodies, the theologians, sociologists, psychologists, exegetes, Church historians, canonists and the Commission for the Revision of Canon Law should sit still. A good example of how fruitful discussion among all kinds of experts on Canon Law can be was the seminar held on the function of law in the Church, organized by the *Canon Law Society of America* at Pittsburgh, October 8-10, 1966, the results of which will soon be published. But such enterprises can only do preparatory work for the time being without aiming at conclusive and definitive legal arrangements. Perhaps I may make some suggestions about this kind of work.

6. *Suggestions*

(a) *More Contact.* If the various bodies that are involved in this work want to do something fruitful, there should be more contact between them. They should not work independently if they want to avoid futility. Would it not be possible, for instance, for the various study groups of the Commission for the Revision of Canon Law to collaborate with those departments of the Roman Curia which have a special competence in matters with which these groups are concerned? This would create a much broader confrontation of experience and insight. Sometimes one department is busy on a specific question while another produces already various measures about which the first was wholly uninformed. This kind of thing is the more regrettable if it is caused by quarrels about competence and one body wants to assert its exclusive competence over against the other. There are differences of competence that are mainly or exclusively concerned with factual interests of the community at large, and the community may be well served by a precise distribution of competence. But when these differences arise merely and exclusively out of the matter of competence itself, they not only show a sad lack of Christian spirit in individual persons but a functional disease in the community. One would also like to see a properly organized system of communication between the bodies that are officially charged with the revision of Church order, and the branch of science whose function it is in the Church to deal with it. It is, for instance, a great pity if a group of the revision commission ignores the publications on matters it is concerned with. And would it not be extremely useful if the results of the work of a commission, when it reaches the more or less definitive stage, were submitted to the various associations of canonists that exist in a number of countries, or to the faculties of Canon Law, or to the Catholic universities, in any case in such a way that many experts from all over the world could make their contribution? It would not seem to be impossible to organize this so that the various regions could make their own contribution systematically and on the spot.

(b) *A Broad Composition of the Work Groups*. Next, I would suggest that the groups that are officially or unofficially involved in this work be composed on as broad a basis as possible, both where variety of qualifications and variety of opinions are concerned. It is bad tactics to base the composition of the groups beforehand more or less on the results about which one has already made up one's mind. The kind of ecclesiastical politics that tries to avoid a free and open discussion between people of different opinions, even those of the "extreme right" and the "extreme left", is doomed to failure in the modern situation. It is also a political mistake. Such a political attitude is bound to become public sooner or later, and public opinion is bound to reject it. But even from the practical point of view it does not need a great deal of experience to see that it is precisely deliberations among men of very varied dispositions which will lead to the best balance and the most solid results as long as these men are qualified and ready to listen to each other. It would even be a great advantage if some outstanding experts in the field of Church order were invited from non-Catholic Christian Churches. One may expect that they would be only too willing and would make an extremely important contribution, not only to the ecumenical aspect of the work but to an understanding of our own Catholic Church order.

(c) *Let Us not Insist on the Whole Code of Canon Law.* I would also urgently suggest that we do not insist in theory on the validity of the existing Code as a whole, apart from the modifications which have already been introduced explicitly and legally. It would indeed be mere theory since in practice many canons have already for a long time fallen into disuse, even before the Council. The revision is so very necessary precisely because this Code had already lost touch with reality at large and with the reality of the Code in particular. One can really no longer insist on the present Code in its totality. The new spirit of the Council is not limited exclusively to the conciliar texts, executive instructions and new laws. It lives in the whole Church in all its manifestations and will continue to express itself in all kinds of genuine Christian and ecclesiastical initiatives which are not—or not yet—to be found in the texts. To maintain the juridical fiction of a still valid Code (apart from positive modifications that have been introduced) in order to cope responsibly and factually with various cases, is fair enough. But it is not reasonable to attack new and justifiable, honest and open initiatives on the ground of existing canons. In matters of Church order and its development we are at the moment far more concerned with the "discernment of the spirits" than with ready-made norms. Study of the norms and reasonable freedom to experiment imply one another. If the new Church order is going to be "real" it can only be so because it has grown out of the reality.

The method of codification of the new Church order must itself be an expression of the new spirit of the Council. In the days when the present Code was being prepared, the projects were worked out secretly and secretly sent to the bishops who had to send in their observations equally in secret. That corresponded to the opinions about Church administration and government of those days. This procedure no longer suits an age when the Church has genuinely accepted collegiality, the responsibility of the whole People of God, the particular character of the local Churches, and so on. The true nature of this codification will not consist of a systematically and technically perfect all-embracing system of legislation. It will consist in a gradual process of decision-taking, a process that will be determined by the progress of the development itself, without superfluous norms, without premature interventions and without *a priori* and unrealistically conceived structures. And this by itself determines its limitations.

✠ Neophytos Edelby/*Damascus, Syria*

Unity or Plurality of Codes: Should the Eastern Churches Have a Special Code?

Since parts of the Eastern Churches have been reunited with Rome, the question has arisen as to whether they should adopt the discipline of the Catholic West or be allowed to keep their own discipline. Theoretically the question of principle has never been a difficulty. All the popes have declared that after reunion the Eastern Churches should remain Eastern and preserve their own spiritual heritage. But if Rome has found it easy to allow differences of liturgy in the East, in practice she has found it harder to allow differences of discipline. The Eastern Christians themselves often thought that Westernization was the right course to follow in reunion with Rome. They usually preserved their liturgical traditions but were less ready to preserve their own discipline and considered that a deepening of their Catholicism implied the fullest possible adoption of Latin discipline.

For their part the popes did not feel they ought to behave any differently toward the Eastern Church, and they maintained their usual Western attitude in this regard. They often intervened in the lives of the Eastern Churches, legislated for them and thus gave rise not to an Eastern law, but to a Roman law for the use of Eastern Christians.

However, the East reacted against this behavior. The strongest resistance to this process of Latinization came from those

Churches whose origin and situation forced them to take into account the reactions of the Orthodox branch of their rite. Thus, generally speaking, Latinization has made far less progress in the Eastern Catholic Churches of the Byzantine rite. With the recent development of the ecumenical movement and the increased awareness of the Eastern Catholic Churches of their mission to the Orthodox, the resistance to Latinization has become stronger. This has resulted in the firm declarations of principle given by Vatican Council II.

The Position Taken by the Council

First of all the Council laid the foundation of the Eastern Churches' own discipline by recognizing *particular Churches* within the Church and declaring that unity is not uniformity in all things: "Moreover, within the Church particular Churches hold a rightful place. These Churches *retain their own traditions* without in any way lessening the primacy of the Chair of Peter. This Chair presides over the whole assembly of charity and *protects legitimate differences;* at the same time it sees that such differences do not hinder unity but rather contribute toward it." [1]

The Council stated this even more clearly in the *Decree on Ecumenism:* "While preserving unity in essentials, let all members of the Church, according to the office entrusted to each, preserve a proper freedom in the various forms of spiritual life and discipline, in the variety of liturgical rights and even in the theological elaborations of revealed truths." [2] Of the Eastern Churches in particular, the *Decree on Ecumenism* insists on the legitimacy of their own discipline and the importance to the union of the Churches that it be preserved: "From the earliest times, moreover, the Eastern Churches followed their own disciplines, sanctioned by the Holy Fathers, by synods and even by ecumenical councils. Far from being an obstacle to the Church's unity, such diversity of customs and observances only adds to her comeliness and contributes greatly to the carrying out of her

[1] *Dogmatic Constitution on the Church,* n. 13.
[2] *Decree on Ecumenism,* n. 4.

mission, as has already been recalled. To remove any shadow of doubt, then, this sacred Synod solemnly declares that the Churches of the East, while keeping in mind the necessary unity of the whole Church, have the power to govern themselves according to their own disciplines, since these are better suited to the temperament of their faithful and better adapted to foster the good of souls. Although it has not always been honored, the strict observance of this traditional principle is among the prerequisites for any restoration of unity." [3]

This principle is applied in a more precise manner to those sectors of the Eastern Churches which have already reunited with Rome. In the *Decree on the Catholic Churches of the Eastern Rite,* the right of these communities to their own discipline is often mentioned: "[The Council] solemnly declares that the Churches of the East, as much as those of the West, fully enjoy the right, and are in duty bound, to rule themselves. Each should do so according to its proper and individual procedures, inasmuch as practices sanctioned by a noble antiquity harmonize better with the customs of the faithful and are seen as more likely to foster the good of souls." [4]

The same Decree further states: "All Eastern rite members should know and be convinced that they can and should always preserve their lawful liturgical rites and their established way of life, and that these should not be altered except by way of an appropriate and organic development." [5]

The Council goes so far as to recommend that Eastern Catholics who have abandoned their own traditions return to them: "If they have improperly fallen away from them because of circumstances of time or personage, let them take pains to return to their ancestral ways." [6] The Council is not content to declare the legitimacy and the obligation of preserving their own discipline; it wants to restore it to its primitive purity, going back past an Eastern law, which to a greater or lesser extent has been

[3] *Ibid.,* n. 16.
[4] *Decree on the Catholic Churches of the Eastern Rite,* n. 5.
[5] *Ibid.,* n. 6.
[6] *Ibid.,* n. 6.

Latinized, to an authentically Eastern law which must nevertheless be capable of appropriate adaptation and organic evolution.
This is the sense in which the other principles of the Council
must be interpreted—the principles of restoration of the rights
and privileges of the patriarchs, "in accord with the ancient
traditions of each Church and the decrees of the ecumenical
Synods" [7] as they were in force "when East and West were in
union",[8] and to consider the patriarchs and their synods as "the
superior authority for all affairs of the patriarchate".[9]

First Attempt at an Eastern Codification

These ideas were vaguely admitted when Pius XI undertook
to grant the Eastern Catholic Churches a special Code on the
model of the *Codex juris canonici*. The latter was taken as the
basis for the work. The compilers diverged from it as little as
possible. The principal advantage of this codification was to
bring to light the ancient disciplines of every Church, and above
all to bring them together, but allowing only a very small place
to the law belonging to each particular Church. For the first
time in history, these Churches, which appeared to have everything to divide them, were united in their discipline. Rome
profited by gaining a modern Code, drawn up by her and common to all the Eastern Churches; the Eastern Churches profited
by acquiring a clear and convenient legislation, known and
respected by the Western bishops who often had many Eastern
Christians not living in the East under their jurisdiction.

The work of codification was sufficiently advanced for Pius
XII to think it proper to publish various parts. In 1949 and
1957 parts of the projected Eastern Code were promulgated in
four Motu Proprios: on marriage, procedure for religious, temporal goods, and rites and the rights of persons. In 1958 other
parts, notably on general norms and sacramental discipline,
were about to be published when Pius XII died. The announce-

[7] *Ibid.*, n. 9.
[8] *Ibid.*
[9] *Ibid.*

ment by John XXIII of the Council, his decision to revise both the Latin and the Eastern Codes, and the opposition, particularly of the Melkites, to the promulgation of the canons on rites and the hierarchy, suspended for a long time the promulgation of the other parts of the Eastern Code.

This first attempt at an Eastern codification has had different judgments passed on it. Technically, it is an improvement on the Latin codification; it has used the Latin and improved on it. In the East it has been criticized in many ways. For the Byzantine Churches it is still too Latin and Latinizing; for the Syrian, Armenian, Coptic and Chaldean Churches, it is too Byzantine. In fact, it is the basis which is at fault, because it has taken the Latin Code for its model. Moreover, Rome has long had the habit of interfering too frequently in the life of these Churches and it was thus difficult for her to imagine a legislation in which the powers of the patriarchs and bishops were not subject to her antecedent or subsequent ratification. Beneath an apparent autonomy, the Eastern patriarchates were treated no differently by Rome than the dioceses of the West.

After the Council this state of affairs could no longer continue. All agreed that a revision was urgently necessary. However, because the Latin Code was again under revision, some canonists wondered whether it might not be convenient to assimilate the two legislations and thus give the Church one single Code which would show sufficient respect to the special conditions in the Eastern Churches.

The question had been raised in 1929 when the Eastern codification began. From our information it appears that the preparatory commission, presided over by Cardinal Gasparri, pronounced in favor of a single Code. The vigorous intervention of Pius XI was necessary to obtain a special compilation for the Eastern Churches.

The question has been raised again by the committee for the revision of the Code of Canon Law: Should there be a single or a double Code? It appears that finally a sort of constitutional Code for the Church will be drawn up which will have to be common to East and West, and then the distinction will be kept between the Latin and the Oriental Code.

Why Should There Be a Separate Code for the East?

The controversy about the double or single Code may become insoluble unless the respective positions are first clarified.

Of course no one imagines that everything will be different in the two legislations. It may even be granted that what is common to the two Codes is more important than what is different in them. At the Council, the emphasis on particular aspects of the spiritual patrimony of the East was so great that the impression was sometimes given that the differences were essential and irreconcilable. If harmony is possible between the Catholics and the Orthodox, it is all the more possible between Catholics of East and West.

Neither does anyone imagine that a constitutional Code for the Church, if it is seen fitting to draw one up, would not be equally applicable to East and West. Furthermore, this single and preliminary Code could also contain the general norms of ecclesiastical law and the norms of the relations between rites that would be applicable in both East and West.

The problem concerns what comes after these constitutional, general and interritual norms: the sacred hierarchy, religious, "things", ecclesiastical procedure, offenses and penalties. Clearly, Eastern and Latin law are sometimes alike and sometimes different in these matters. Should there be a single Code in which the Eastern divergences are noted, or should there be two distinct Codes, even though they will sometimes overlap?

There can be no doubt that a single Code has certain advantages, particularly practical ones. A single Code would link the Eastern and Western Churches more closely. The Eastern divergences would be mentioned in it and this might even emphasize them more strongly. All Catholics would have the same Code. The Eastern Catholics would become familiar with Latin discipline, and Western Catholics could no longer remain ignorant of that of the East.

However, all things considered, these advantages of a single Code are outweighed by the practical inconveniences and some very important ecumenical considerations:

1. In the first place it is irritating and fundamentally unjust always to present the Eastern divergences as exceptions to the common rule. The Latin Church, however large, is no less a particular Church than the smallest of Eastern Churches. The Latin Roman Church and the Catholic Church are not identical. It is therefore false to consider the law of the Latin Church as the common law of the Catholic Church, and the law of the Eastern Churches as a peculiar, special and exceptional law. This would be bound to happen if a single Code was drawn up, unless there were a particular Code for the Latin Church and another particular Code for the Eastern Churches—but then there would in fact be two Codes even though they were printed in a single volume, and it would be incorrect in this case to speak of a *fusion* of the two Codes; it would be a juxtaposition.

2. Second, those who were entrusted *now* with drawing up a single Code for the two Churches *would not be able to avoid Latinizing Eastern law*. The Latinizing tendency is so widespread that even the best Eastern canonists at the present time are only conversant with Latin law or with Latin-Eastern law— which is to say a law fundamentally Latin, but dotted with Eastern terminology here and there. It could not be otherwise because their sources are the acts and decrees of the Roman pontiffs, which is a very different thing from Oriental law or the particular legislations of each Oriental community which long ago fell away from the authentic Eastern tradition under the influence of Latin law. This can be shown merely by reading the acts of the Eastern Catholic synods during the last two centuries; almost without exception they are exact replicas of the synods held in the West over the same period.

3. Third, a single codification has a built-in tendency *to sacrifice as much as possible of the differences in Eastern law* and thus Latinize it even more. A single Code can only be suitable if the exceptions are reduced to the minimum. When-

ever the codifiers are faced with two usages, they will be tempted, for the sake of conformity, not to adjust the Western law to the Oriental usage but rather to do the opposite. Rome's attempt to codify Eastern law showed how dangerous it is simply to take Latin law as a basis, and it would clearly be even more dangerous to try and fuse the Eastern and the Latin in a single Code.

4. Fourth, it should not be forgotten that the Eastern Code, even though properly speaking it will apply only to Eastern Catholics, must reflect the deep-rooted attitude of the Catholic Church in her dialogue with the Orthodox. It is generally admitted that if the Orthodox Churches are one day to reestablish communion with Rome, it will be by way of the Eastern Churches already reunited or by the canonical status—still unsatisfactory but improving—granted them within the Catholic Church. Nevertheless, the way Eastern Catholics are treated cannot fail to influence the reaction of Orthodox Christians to all approaches by the Catholic Church. The late Cardinal Massimi, who had replaced Cardinal Coussa and was the guiding spirit of the Eastern codification, said one day to the Melkite patriarch, Cyril IX: "We want the Orthodox to say when they see our codification: 'This is our Eastern law.'" The intention was admirable and sincere, but the results fell far short. It could not have been otherwise.

An Eastern Code, even if drawn up only for Eastern Catholics, must consider ecumenism as its first concern. It should go beyond the stage of "uniatism" and beyond the existing Eastern Catholic communities which are essentially provisional and prepare a state of affairs in which the Orthodox and the Catholic can be comfortably reunited. We may even say that the Eastern codification will not have achieved its end until it has become superfluous and the reunion of Orthodox and Catholic makes the continued existence of the present Eastern Catholic communities unnecessary. This clearly cannot be achieved by a single Code for the Roman Church and the Eastern Catholic Churches.

5. Finally, if the fusion of the two Codes has up to now

been a difficult and undesirable task, it has become *morally impossible* since the Council. It should not be forgotten that Vatican Council II, in a small section of the *Decree on the Catholic Churches of the Eastern Rite,* hardly noticed by the public, laid down a principle of the utmost importance for the life of the Eastern Catholics and for the future of the dialogue with the Orthodox: the principle of the internal disciplinary autonomy of the Eastern Churches. It reads: "The patriarchs with their synods constitute the superior authority[10] for all affairs of the patriarchate, including the right to establish new eparchies and to nominate bishops of their rite within the territorial bounds of the patriarchate, without prejudice to the inalienable right of the Roman pontiff to intervene in individual cases" (n. 9).

This principle will revolutionize all current Eastern discipline. The pope *can* always intervene if it is necessary for the good of the Church, *but he never has to intervene.* Henceforth the Eastern Churches are to govern themselves as they did during the thousand years of union. It will require a reason of public importance, at the discretion of the pope, for an intervention on his part in a particular case. This is a far cry from the present setup in which patriarchs, bishops and synods can do precious little without previous or subsequent ratification by Rome. One may well wonder how many of the present canons of Eastern discipline actually remain in force after this Council Decree.

If this principle is truly applied, it must revolutionize the structure of all future Eastern codification, making the fusions of the two Codes less viable than ever.

Why a Single Eastern Code?

This canonical autonomy should not go so far as to induce each Eastern Church to draw up its own Code. It is right that each Church should have its special law—that is, in matters of usage of secondary importance, where there would be no point

[10] Not "supreme" which properly describes only ecumenical councils and popes. "Chief court" signifies the court which is *normally* the ultimately responsible, not excluding a higher court but acting in the last resort without necessarily referring to it.

in uniformity. However, all the Eastern Catholic Churches should have one single Code.

In fact, although the Eastern Churches are sufficiently different from the Western Church to have a right to their own Code, they have sufficient disciplinary affinities to make it proper for them to share a single Code, which would nevertheless respect differences between rites under "special law".

There would thus exist in the Catholic Church a triple body of legislation:

1. A Code of general law, which could be called the constitutional or organic Code, containing general norms and norms for interritual relations. This Code would be common to Eastern and Latin Churches.

2. Two particular Codes of ecclesiastical law, one for the Latin Church, the other for all the Eastern Catholic Churches. These Codes may sometimes overlap. However, the Eastern Code should not take the Latin Code as its basis; its inspiration should be profoundly ecumenical; it would be of a provisional character, adapted to the present situation of the communities for which it is designed, and bearing in mind the small number of their faithful and their peculiar position. It will be as close as possible to the corresponding law of their Orthodox brothers. It will take particular care to respect the new canonical status granted the Eastern Churches by Vatican Council II: return to their authentic Eastern discipline; restoration of the rights and prerogatives of the patriarchs to what they were during the thousand years of union; possibility of a harmonious organic evolution; internal canonical autonomy allowing for the intervention of the pope when he sees fit to intervene in a particular case but not *necessarily* requiring recourse to Rome either before or afterward. This would be a single Code for all the Eastern Catholic Churches. An attempt to draw up a Code for each would cause enormous confusion and would hinder vital collaboration between them. This single Code should be drawn up by really competent Eastern canonists, who believe in the spirit of the Council, and be helped by Western colleagues, well versed not

in the hybrid Latin-Eastern law of recent times but in authentic Eastern law, who respected the East and who believed in their mission and were anxious to give brotherly assistance. This single Eastern Code would be simultaneously promulgated by the supreme legislative authority in each particular Church.

3. Finally, the necessary number of special Codes for each Eastern and Western Church (the various episcopal conferences) would compile their own usages on points with which the single Code had not dealt. These special Codes would naturally be drawn up and promulgated by each particular Church.

This is the way, we think, to meet the need of the Eastern Churches for unity and simplification and their legitimate wish to remain authentic, not through the mere desire to be different but in order to accomplish their mission and better serve their faithful.[11]

[11] For further study of this subject, cf. M. Breydy, "Dialogo canonico entre orientales y occidentales," in *Estudios de Deusto* IX (1961), pp. 140-50; I. Ziadeh, "Sur la necessité d'un code unique de droit canonique pour l'Eglise," in *Antiochena* 6 (1965), pp. 11-14 (English translation in *One in Christ* 2 [1966], pp. 70-4; the same study was adapted and developed in *L'Orient syrien* XI [1966], pp. 90-8, with a further note in *Antiochena* 8 [1965], pp. 23-4); M. Doumith, "De l'unité du code de droit dans l'Eglise catholique," in *Antiochena* 7 (1965), pp. 23-7; Patriarch Maximos IV, "Contre le projet d'un code unique pour l'église orientale et l'église occidentale," in *L'Eglise grecque-melkite au concile* (Beyrout, 1967), pp. 505-7.

Peter Shannon/*Chicago, Illinois*

The Code of Canon Law: 1918-1967

Two days ago, it began to snow here in Chicago—beautiful white flakes floating serenely from the heavens upon our homes and streets and trees. The snow has continued to fall. It still looks beautiful, it is beautiful, but it is also crippling and devastating. All roads are impassable. Thousands are marooned. A huge city is paralyzed.

Fifty years ago some brilliant men, under the direction of Cardinal Gasparri, wrote a book of rules or canons, some 2,414 canons. These canons, like the snowflakes, looked beautiful, and in a sense, are beautiful. Most canon lawyers admit that Gasparri and his associates brought order out of chaos, the chaos of nineteen centuries of disparate, obscure, often unintelligible Church laws. As a Code of Law, Gasparri's work is a masterpiece—precise, clear, complete. Yet this same Code of Law has in some ways over the last fifty years partially disabled the city of God. What seemed a thing of beauty has quite often proved a liability, rather than an asset. The Code, which Pius X and Gasparri knew would bring to the Church a greater unity through law, unwittingly also brought into the Church a crippling uniformity. It wasn't the fault of Pius X, or Benedict XV, or Gasparri. It was nobody's fault, and yet it was everyone's fault.

I have been assigned to analyze the Code's effectiveness over the past fifty years. A thorough analysis would demand a series of books, rather than an article such as this. It is my opinion that as a legal order or system, the Code leaves much to be desired, although obviously some aspects of the Code are commendable. Four reasons, which I shall comment upon briefly, may perhaps explain the basis for my criticism of Canon Law in general and the Code of Canon Law in particular.

1. *A Seeming Unawareness of Basic Theology*

Theology, the study of the existence, nature and laws of God, is concerned with the twofold relationship between a God who invites and man who responds. Man's response, basically through service of his fellow man, must be a human response, autonomous and free. Man chooses, wills, loves and acts "ab intra"; otherwise he ceases to be a rational creature, and his ability to respond to God's invitation is destroyed.

Some individual canons within the Code do in fact maintain and defend man's autonomy, but the Code as a whole envisions man as a creature to be directed (manipulated?) through law, directed by the Church or rather by the authorities within the Church. This vision of man was undoubtedly predicated on the assumption that the "common man" needs to be led, that he must be told exactly what to do, exactly how to respond. Thus the law multiplied, often at the expense of individual freedom. This multiplication of laws is noticeable not only in the history of Canon Law but also in the history of civil law, particularly the history of European law. The redactors of the Code were imbued with the 19th-century European legal tradition and they sought, through a complete codification of Canon Law, to regulate the bulk of man's activities.

Many believe that the Code tries to direct man "ab extra" toward his eternal goal and some feel that the Code is primarily a cudgel to keep man in line, to keep him from straying too far from the "sure" road to heaven.

Canon Law and theology are two distinct sciences, but the former, even though distinct, must serve the latter. Unless Canon Law sinks its roots in current as well as traditional theology, it fails to deal with the reality of man and the reality of the risen Christ communicating his Spirit to the community. Twentieth-century theology insists that Christianity is a call to greater freedom. Twentieth-century Canon Law should not inhibit that freedom, unless absolutely necessary.

2. *A Regrettable Ignorance of Ecclesiology*

Pope John and Vatican Council II did not appear on the scene until forty years after the Code. Thus Gasparri and company had some excuse for considering the Church almost exclusively as a hierarchical institution. One might not expect to find in the Code expressions such as "the People of God", or "the family of God", but surely the concept of equality within the Church should have permeated the Code. Yet nowhere in the Code do we find such a concept.

Christ's Church was indeed founded on authority, the authority of the risen Christ conferred primarily on the pope and the bishops. But this authority is to be exercised through service of the people, who are, always were and always will be of paramount importance to the God-Man. And the "people" for whom the God-Man died and arose and to whom he now communicates the Spirit are the people of the entire world, not simply Christians, much less Catholics. All canonists today, I believe, admit that the Code, in its provisions with respect to non-Catholics, evidences a lack of pastoral concern. Some canonists, moreover, maintain that the Code implicitly equates non-Catholics with the un-saved, who become saved when and if they are by the grace of God converted to Catholicism.

Even the "simple" people within the Church—laity, Religious and curates—are accorded few rights by the Code. Always the emphasis is placed on obedience, generally blind obedience, whereas love, the love of neighbor, is relegated to second place among the virtues and commands of Christ. Always the institution, the hierarchical institution, is given precedence over the person. Little wonder that millions of Christians fail to recognize the Catholic Church as the Church of Christ. Little wonder that millions of non-Christians either hate or ignore the Catholic Church. The Code should not be made the scapegoat for our Church of isolation, but it can be charged with some responsibility for separating, isolating, ghetto-izing Catholics. For the Code does view the world as evil and the Code does consider non-Catholics as people to be avoided.

One may envision the above criticism as extreme, and perhaps it is. The question, however, is not whether such criticism is extreme, but whether it is merited. Too long have we canonists sought to defend, rather than rebuild, a vulnerable legal order; too long have we gone along with a Code that fails to reflect our 20th-century understanding of the Church; too long have we administered the law "objectively" without consideration for the circumstances, the existential situation, the "subject" of the law; too long have we allowed some institutions within the Church to discipline, silence or crush critics of the system.

The Code has been criticized by ecclesiologists for categorizing sacraments as "things" ("res"); it has been criticized by spiritual directors for so detailing the law for Religious that religious profession is considered in some circles as an abandonment of creativity. It has been criticized by bishops for complicating the procedural law of marriage, thus according only a relative handful of deserving petitioners a just hearing in the course of a year. It has been criticized by priests for devoting an entire book containing 220 canons to penal law, thus giving rise to the impression that the essence of Canon Law is "coercion" rather than "authority". These critics cannot be dismissed as "extremists" or "angry young men".

The only question today is not whether such criticism of the Code is excessive, but only whether it is prudent to speak or write openly and honestly at this particular time. I think such criticism should be made, because I fear that unless the entire Christian Community is made aware of the inequity of our present law, unless the entire Christian Community is aroused, unless the entire Christian Community is shaken from its complacency, unless the entire Christian Community realizes its responsibility to the world, then in the near future we may be faced with a new Code hardly different than our present one. Such a Code would be a tragedy, not just for the Church, but for all mankind.

3. *An Emphasis on Centralization rather than Subsidiarity*

The principle of subsidiarity, as formulated by Pius XI in *Quadragesimo Anno* and enshrined by Pope John XXIII in *Mater et Magistra*, reads: "This supremely important principle of social philosophy, one which cannot be set aside or altered, remains firm and unshaken: Just as it is wrong to withdraw from the individual and commit to the community at large what private enterprise and endeavor can accomplish, so it is likewise unjust and a gravely harmful disturbance of right order to turn over to a greater society of higher rank functions and services, which can be performed by lesser bodies on a lower plane. For a social undertaking of any sort, by its very nature, ought to aid the members of the body social, but never to destroy and absorb them." [1]

The Code has produced a blueprint of detailed, centralized legislation, directly contrary to, if not contradictory of, the principle of subsidiarity. The Code gravely violated subsidiarity and unfortunately the situation has worsened since the Code. Roman Congregations have jealously guarded and systematically enhanced their prerogatives. Hundreds of directives, bearing the force of law, have been sent by the Roman Curia to the bishops, with the result that greater centralization has occurred and many "laws" have been promulgated outside the Code. The influence of the Curia reaches into every country through the outdated system of papal nunciatures and apostolic delegations, which, in many instances, have more power and authority than any individual bishop or even than a National Episcopal Conference.

Dispensations and privileges have proliferated, requiring an appeal to higher authority before performing a commonplace action. A bishop must appeal to Rome or the Nunciature for

[1] *Acta Apost. Sedis*, 23 (1931), 203; 53 (1961), 414.

permission to spend more than $5,000, a pastor must ask his bishop for permission to dispense with the reading of marriage banns, a curate must request the pastor for permission to dispense a parishioner from the law of fast and abstinence, a nun must ask her superior for permission to leave the convent in order to partake of the sacrament of penance, a layman must obtain permission from his pastor or bishop to act as witness to a sacramental marriage in a Protestant church.

A certain amount of centralization is necessary in any visible society, and the Church is indeed a visible society. But the constant necessity of obtaining a dispensation, a rescript, a privilege from a higher authority before one can act disregards the principle of subsidiarity and belies the dignity of man.

The situation would not seem so restrictive if those seeking permission felt that those empowered to grant permission actually knew the local situation. But parishioners wonder if their pastors, particularly pastors of large, urban parishes, really know and understand them. Priests wonder if bishops, particularly bishops immersed in administration, really understand the pastoral needs of their people, priests, Religious and laity. Americans, Africans and Australians wonder if priests, working in the Roman Curia, have more than a superficial knowledge of the culture, customs and needs of the people in an individual country, other than Italy.

Lest we be accused of speaking in generalities, let me describe a case which is all too familiar and painful for American priests. Lizzie Smith, a Negro girl of fifteen, marries a seventeen-year-old boy in Mississippi. The marriage lasts some two months, until Lizzie and her husband realize that they really didn't understand what marriage is all about. Five years later Lizzie moves to New York, Chicago or Los Angeles, where she meets and falls in love with a good man. They marry and now have five children, all of whom are being reared as Catholics. Lizzie and her present husband have both completed instructions in the Catholic religion, attend Mass regularly and wish to become Catholics themselves. Fortunately Lizzie was never baptized, so her parish priest knows he can refer her to the local matrimonial tribunal, where she may or may not receive a fair hearing, and where her case may or may not be swiftly processed. A "swift process" means that the local tribunal in three months time has managed to interview Lizzie and her relatives, has tried to locate and interview Lizzie's former husband, has obtained character witnesses for Lizzie and her relatives (the law says character witnesses should be Catholic, apparently because non-Catholics are presumed to prevaricate), has received a letter of commendation from Lizzie's pastor, has checked the baptismal records of every Protestant church ever attended by Lizzie, has typed all the Acts of the case and drafted a lengthy opinion on the case to be signed by the bishop. After such a "swift process", Lizzie's case is forwarded to the Sacred Congregation for the Doctrine of Faith (formerly the Holy Office), where it will be examined and judged by a tribunal of three priests, who decide whether it is true that Lizzie was never baptized. If the proof is there, the case is a simple one, and the Holy Father is duly requested to dissolve the bond of Lizzie's first marriage in favor of the Faith. This "swift process" somehow is slowed down in Rome, slowed down so much that thirteen more months elapse before any decision is issued—a decision, mind you, that is based entirely on one fact—whether or not Lizzie was baptized. All the time, Lizzie's parish priest is probably wondering why he couldn't simply take Lizzie's word or the word of her parents; all the time, the local tribunal, which obtained the evidence and checked the churches, is probably wondering why a Roman tribunal is any more competent than the local tribunal to judge a simple question of baptism or non-baptism; all the time, Lizzie's children are wondering why their parents cannot participate in the eucharist; all the time, Lizzie and her husband are wondering why the Church won't let them become Catholics. The above case of Lizzie is a relatively simple one and a case that will eventually have a happy ending. But there are thousands of equally deserving cases that do not have a happy ending, because the involved procedure demanded by law is so complicated that only the largest dioceses have sufficient manpower to process such cases. Worse still, parish priests often are so disgusted with the "red tape" that they don't bother even referring people to the local tribunal.

The so-called "Privilege of the Faith", into which category Lizzie's case fell, is no isolated example of the violation of subsidiarity. The entire procedural law of marriage violates subsidiarity, as do whole sections of the law for religious and penal law.

4. *An Unevangelical Overemphasis on the Letter of the Law*

Salvation history, culminating in the redemption by the God-Man, reveals a God who is faithful and merciful, faithful to his people, merciful to sinners. The Church founded by Christ is meant to reflect in a visible way that same fidelity and mercy, for the Church is the body of Christ.

It would seem that Church Law should also, in some way, reflect Christ's love for the world, his mercy, his fidelity. In a word, Church Law should be charismatic, a sign to the world that the risen Christ is still communicating to men, through his Spirit, the divine mercy and love that characterized his life on earth. Church Law, therefore, should lead men to Jesus.

The Code, however, through its peculiar mixture of authoritarianism and paternalism can only turn men away from the Church and thus, in a true sense, turn men away from Christ. Since the Church is or should be a community of love, I wonder whether Church Law might better be formulated in a language of love—in a pastoral rather than dogmatic, in a hortatory rather than commanding tone. I well realize the difficulty of expressing law in non-legal terms, of encouraging and advising rather than commanding. On the other hand, how does one command love? Can the Church so circumscribe man's external actions through law, that man has no other choice than to love the Lord God with his whole soul and love his neighbor as himself? Certainly Canon Law can facilitate the exchange of love between man and his neighbor, but love itself must be a free, human response. Otherwise "love" is tokenism or hypocrisy, but not love.

I submit that the Code is so structured and the Canons so formulated that man is commanded to observe the letter of the law, while at the same time the Code places little emphasis on observing the spirit of the law. One principle underlying the formulation of the Canons is that the reason for the law need not and should not be included in the law. (*Ratio legis non cadit sub lege.*) Such a principle has led many Catholics to equate external observance of the law with true observance of the law. Obedience to the letter of the law seems to have been substituted for love of God and love of neighbor, causing one seminarian to remark facetiously: "By this shall all men know that you are my disciples, if you learn and obey my 2,414 rules of law." [2]

I hope to see the day when the Church will develop a universal, constitutional law based on the dignity and rights of all the people of God. I hope to see the day when the Church will permit a nation or region to build a legal order based on the culture of that region. I hope to see the day when theology and ecclesiology will determine the law rather than vice versa. I hope to see the day when all—priests, Religious, laity, psychologists, sociologists, anthropologists, etc.—will have a real voice in determining the law. I hope to see the day when a canon lawyer like myself can look at the law and say: "Here is reflected the love of Christ", instead of saying, as I now do in looking at the law: "Woe to us lawyers who load men with burdens they can hardly carry."

[2] Cf. Luke 11, 46.

Hans Heimerl/*Graz, Austria*

Outline of a Constitution for the Church

In modern discussion about the reform of the Code of Canon Law the idea has emerged of a constitution for the Church which would be common and basic to the whole Church, both Latin and Eastern. This possibility was also mentioned by Pope Paul himself to the Commission for the Revision of Canon Law on November 20, 1965.[1] This idea gives rise to two tendencies that do not quite cover each other. On the one hand, one could lay down an identical and common legal foundation for all parts of the Church, at present for both the Latin and Eastern Churches, but in the future also for Churches of the West with a different character. On the other hand, there is the model of political constitutions in the modern State which fix the basic legal structure and in particular ensure the fundamental rights of the individual. And so we have to face the preliminary question whether an analogous legal set-up would be justified in the Church.

The Specific Character of an Ecclesiastical Constitution

The general theory of Church law wavers today between the extremes of "de-theologizing" it and "de-legalizing" it. There is, however, increasing acceptance of the fact that Church law must correspond to the nature of the Church, and this, according to

[1] *Acta Apost. Sedis* 57 (1965), p. 988.

Vatican Council II, is a complex reality composed of both human and divine elements.[2] Church law is, therefore, genuine law, as it is also found in other human societies, while it is at the same time penetrated by the law of Christ and his Spirit who operates in the Church. Therefore, it is quite possible for a constitution for the Church to let itself be inspired by political constitutions, particularly insofar as juridical procedure and the matters to be dealt with are concerned. But there are limits to this. The basic idea of the sovereignty of the people cannot be taken over by a Church constitution because it is not rooted in the people, nor, fundamentally, in the ecclesiastical authorities, but in Christ himself. It is determined by the spiritual character of the one government that represents Christ as priest, shepherd and prophet, and not so much by the distribution of power that is common to the constitution of the modern State. The organization of the offices is largely predetermined by divine right. An eventual constitution should primarily and ultimately ensure only spiritual rights or matters of that nature. Finally, it should be made clear over against positivist tendencies that the Church had her constitution from the beginning and that all a constitutional Code can do is to formulate it and to give it further precision.

The specific nature of an ecclesiastical constitution must be particularly clear in the attitude it takes to the issue of democracy in the Church. No democratic principles or forms can be bodily applied to the Church, nor can one condemn the whole democratic approach just like that and eliminate it from the Church. It is much more a matter of allowing full play to the new lines of thought about the Christian value of service, collegiality and brotherhood in the field of Church law, as the Council started this process. If this gives rise to an apparently large number of democratic processes, they are the fruit of the Church's own Spirit and essentially distinct from similar phenomena in secular society.

While political constitutions were often inspired by the need

[2] *De Ecclesia*, n. 8.

to limit the absolute power of the monarch, we must maintain that the full power of the papacy cannot be limited more by an ecclesiastical constitution than is already done by divine law. But it is in no way beyond a constitution of the Church to transfer many cases of exclusively papal competence in the present situation to other bodies. Even present law binds the pope normally to respect a number of pre-conditions and pro-cedures as well as existing rights without in any way diminishing his supreme jurisdiction.

The Content and the Scope of Constitutional Validity

The constitution should be planned so as to be valid for all parts of the Church. This universalist scope of its validity can be understood in different ways and should be a guide for what it should contain, i.e., the quantity of matters to be legislated upon and the thoroughness of this legislation.

In the strictest sense one could plan a Code that would be stripped of all excessive detail and would thereby leave room for local or particular laws. In this case the constitution would be wide in scope and cover all the matter that has up till now been treated in the Code, though it would deal with this matter in less detail. Such a Code would then go beyond what is usually meant by a constitution: it could exist side by side with such a constitution but not replace it. Such a generalized Code would only be valid for the Latin Church, like the present one.

A constitutional Code is usually thought of as valid for both the Latin Church and the Eastern Catholic Churches as they now are. Such a Code should not be too all-embracing. Even today there is no strictly common (purely ecclesiastical) law but only a Latin Code along with those parts of an Oriental Code that have so far been promulgated. Yet this Oriental Code has substantially the same law as the Western Church, a fact that has often provoked the displeasure of the Orientals. If then a constitution is to be formally valid for the whole Church, it must at least materially leave wide room for differences and therefore rest satisfied with the essentials that both Churches have in common.

But even such a constitution would not suit the present-day Church, a Church that is looking forward to the unity of all Christians. Even if such a unity of large groups or Churches is not likely to take place in the immediate future, the Catholic Church should formulate its laws already in such a way that it will not obstruct such a reunion. The constitution should really be the constitution of the whole Catholic Church, not only covering the various parts ("rites"), but, beyond that, ecumenical in the sense that it stands open beforehand to all the Christian communions that seek reunion. When the *Decree on the Eastern Churches* states: "If any separated Eastern Christian should . . . join himself to Catholic unity, no more should be required of him than what a simple profession of the Catholic faith demands," [3] this should be reflected in Church law. Such an ecumenically orientated constitution should therefore limit itself to a few basic principles.

These reflections on the scope and validity of a constitution provide us already with a few directives for its content.

The Content

The universalist constitution should contain the norms laid down by divine right about the structure of the Church. Beyond this it should also contain a fair amount of what is not, or at least not plainly, of divine right, but can be considered traditionally as substantially common to both East and West, as well as all those things, including new legal institutions, that are necessary to ensure the organization of the Church.

The constitution should start from the over-all structure of the Church as presented in the first two chapters of the *Constitution on the Church*, i.e., from the organic structure of the People of God, not merely on the basis of hierarchic government but also on the basis of the variety of other graces and callings so that the

[3] *De Eccl. orient. cath.*, n. 25.

Church appears as the unity of an active collectivity of all its members. In this framework there is room for two large sections on the ecclesiastical communities and their administration, and on the basic rights and duties of the members.

The section on the ecclesiastical communities and their administration corresponds in some way to what until now was understood by constitution, but rather from the point of view of the communities than from that of the offices. First, there should be principles that concern the unity of Church government, as taking the place of Christ and as a service to the People of God, and the subsidiary principle in the Church. This naturally determines the rest of this article.

1. *The Universal Church and Its Government:* The pope and the episcopal college; the episcopal synod as the advisory body for the pope in matters of the universal Church; the regulations concerning papal elections; a minimum about the bodies that are in charge of the universal Church. For ecumenical reasons one cannot expect that Churches that want to join the Catholic Church accept a large number of Congregations, offices and tribunals of the Roman Curia. As a necessary minimum in the way of auxiliary and executive bodies one might consider a papal chancery, possibly under another name than the "loaded" one of "curia", together with secretariats to deal with the outward relations of the Church (for Christian unity, for non-Christians, non-believers, and the Secretariat of State), insofar as the "particular" Churches do not deal with this themselves (the Eastern patriarchs can already conclude concordates). We should seriously consider the setting up of a universal constitutional tribunal in order to decide conflicts of constitutional interpretation and to protect the rights laid down in the constitution.

2. *The Particular Churches and Their Government:* The concept of "particular Church" (*ecclesia particularis*) has been been elaborated in the *Decree on the Eastern Churches.* It consists of a number of dioceses, distinguished from other particular Churches by their own hierarchy, their own law, their own liturgy and their own spiritual heritage, and is also designated

by the term "rite" in the broader canonical sense.[4] This variety
of particular Churches brings out the unity of the universal
Church in pluriformity. This particular Church is going to be a
key concept for the Church's constitution because it can provide
the framework for these separate Churches that want to join
the Catholic Church. Such a Church is integrated in the universal Church and is bound by its constitution, but within its
own scope it is, in the right sense of the word, autonomous, i.e.,
it lives according to its own legitimate organization, just as the
present Code works in the particular Latin Church. Such a
particular basic law determines who governs the particular
Church, and how (the patriarch, the primate, the pope as "Patriarch of the West") and what kind of union will bind the local
Churches within the particular Church (ecclesiastical provinces,
new regions to be created still, episcopal conferences). The universalist constitution, on the other hand, will have to determine
in greater detail the relations of the particular Churches with the
primatial government, and lay down what matters should be
normally reserved to the Apostolic See in one form or another.

3. *Local Churches and Their Components:* By "local Church"
is meant the diocese under its bishop, as part of the People of
God. Although integrated in the "particular Church" it must
nevertheless find a place in the general constitution of the universal Church because it is governed by the bishop who has
a function by divine right and because the institution of the
local Church goes back in any case to the first days of Christianity. It must therefore have some degree of autonomy from the
start with regard to the higher levels of authority. What this consists of, how the bishops are appointed, the organization of diocesan government and judicature, advisory bodies, if necessary
with lay participation, territorial and personal organization and
similar details remain subject to the law prevailing in the particular Church, together with the organization of the component elements of the local Church (deaneries, parishes, communities

---

[4] *Ibid.,* nn.4f. In other places "particular Church" refers to the diocese,
i.e., the "local" Church.

based on categories of persons). But the *priests* and *deacons*, who are sacramentally ordained collaborators of the bishop, are a permanent element of the universal Church and by the same token incorporated in the general constitution.

If the particular Churches enjoy wider juridical autonomy, the regulation of their mutual relations becomes the more important. The general constitution must not only recognize their autonomy and equality in principle but also in actual fact.[5] This will bring about a genuine community of worship and sacraments which, however, has certain limits in order to avoid unseemly confusion or absorption. The change-over from one particular Church to another (change of "rite") should be prevented as far as possible, for the same reasons; the coexistence of several particular Churches within one territory can give rise to a great deal of friction and demands cooperation. This kind of problem of what is called "inter-ritual" law has to be dealt with by the constitution.

A constitution for the Church would be incomplete if it were limited to a mere statute of organization, a "hierarchology" It should rather aim at being a comprehensive constitution of the whole ecclesiastical community and therefore also treat of the individual members, their basic rights and duties. Church membership in the juridical sense should be limited to Catholics and the fiction that non-Catholic Christians are bound by Church laws should be abandoned. (The connection with separated Christians falls into a different category of problems.) Among the basic rights of the Christian the first is his right to "spiritual goods", that is, the Word of God, the reception of the sacraments and the pastoral care of the hierarchy. (How necessary it is to formulate this right is evident from limitations of the right to baptism and confirmation introduced recently for important reasons, yet juridically questionable.)

His positive rights concern his cooperation in the shaping of

[5] K. Mörsdorf, "Streiflichter zur Reform des kanonischen Rechtes," in *Arch. f. kath. Kirchenrecht* 135 (1966), pp. 47f., points out that, in spite of the principle of equality solemnly pronounced at Vatican Council II, the Eastern Churches are treated as an "exception".

the Church's life: the right to participate in the liturgy, to confess and spread the faith, to the apostolate, to free expression of opinion in public and with regard to the hierarchy; the right to take the initiative in certain enterprises;[6] to free association for religious purposes;[7] the basic competence to be entrusted by the hierarchy with specifically ecclesiastical tasks and services and to serve on advisory bodies; the right to be free in the choice of sacred orders or marriage or another ecclesiastically significant calling, including that of the "secular state" (*Weltstandes*). Every Christian is entitled to the protection of his rights by legal or governmental bodies, where only one sequence of appeals can ensure this protection. (Whether an appeal from the highest authority in the particular Church to the pope is possible is a delicate question; apparently not normally in the sense of the *Decree on the Eastern Churches*.[8] When accused he has a right to be heard and to defend himself.)

It is obvious that these rights can only be limited insofar as the common good of the Church demands it. One ought to beware of the idea that once these basic rights are fixed by law, we have an exhaustive list of *all* rights. The rights and the freedom of the Christian exist before, and are above, positive Church law.

The basic duties of a Catholic are among other things: participation in Church worship, in the apostolate and the confession of the faith (here seen, not as a right but as a duty), obedience in faith, obedience to the teaching authority of the Church; obedience to the law and the duty to assist the Church in her material needs. None of these duties is unlimited but they are determined by the demands of the common good.

It may surprise the reader that I have not said more about the frequently demanded "law for the laity". But it is now more and more accepted that the lay person (in the true sense of the word) is the "normal" Christian while the clergy with their

---

[6] Cf. *De Ecclesia*, n. 37.

[7] Cf. *De Apostolatu laicorum*, n. 19d and 24c.

[8] *De Eccl. orient. cath.*, n. 9d.

special tasks and powers are the exception; that therefore the rights of the laity are quite simply the rights of the member of the Church; on the other hand, some understand the lay person as the Christian-in-the-world who as such has his particular vocation in the world and is called to a variety of secular tasks and services. In this sense the laity needs no more nor less mention in the constitution as other (less numerous) callings, such as members of religious orders or Christians with a special service. The organization of all these groups of faithful like the matter of clerical status should be left to the particular Church.

Finally, a section of the Church constitution should be devoted to the Church's relations with the outside world. For this the Council has provided plenty of matter: the statements of the *Constitution on the Church* about the relations of the Church with separated Christians, non-Christians and non-believers; the *Decree on the Eastern Churches,* the *Decree on Ecumenism;* the *Declaration on Religious Freedom,* and the *Pastoral Constitution on the Church in the Modern World.* From these one could derive the juridical principles about the relations of the Catholic Church with other Christian communities and their members, with non-Christians and non-believers, and also with States and the commonwealth of nations.

The Form of the Constitution and Its Relation to Other Laws

The outline of the Church's constitution as presented above makes it clear that the language has to be legal language but sufficiently transparent to let the basic theology of the Church come through. It should be limited to what is fundamental and not go into detail. Norms of a constitutional nature but which would exceed this framework, like papal elections, the statutes of the episcopal synod, etc., should be promulgated as laws in their own right, perhaps as an appendix to the constitution. Together with the constitution these laws would then form the constitutional Code. Constitutional law should have priority over all other laws. Ordinary laws concerned with the universal Church but without being strictly part of the constitution should not be incorporated because this would run counter to the principle of pluriformity in unity and the real meaning of a universal constitutional law. Any particular laws should be consonant with the constitution and can indeed be so without losing their particular character which is guaranteed by the constitution.

In this way Church law would have the following order: (1) the constitutional law of the universal Church with its accompanying laws; (2) the constitution and remaining law of the particular Churches; (3) legal definitions of larger units within the particular Church (e.g., provincial synods or episcopal conferences); (4) diocesan law. These various levels might look like splitting up the unity of the present Code, but the only new element is really the constitutional law for the universal Church, as the other sections were already in existence, although dominated by concentration on the law of one particular Church seen as a whole, e.g., in the present Code. There are advantages in preserving this over-concentration on the whole because it would preserve a broad unity, corresponding to the present situation, and also the pluriformity of the universal Church. If the document of the constitution could incorporate an important part of the codification for every particular Church, there would be no less cohesion in the Code than has been the case till now.

What advantage would accrue from such a constitution for the Church? It would put the function of the universal Church with regard to its particular Churches in the right light, as well as bring out the unity-in-pluriformity and the catholicity of the Church. The legal position of various ecclesiastical structures and of the individual member would gain in clarity and security. The clearer perception that Vatican Council II brought to the Church of her own nature would be reflected and fulfilled at the juridical level.

Paul Boyle, C.P./*St. Meinrad, Indiana*

The Renewal of Canon Law and the Resolutions of the Canon Law Society of America, 1965

There is widespread recognition of the need for a renewal in Canon Law and an earnest desire that it be initiated quickly. Many have expressed the hope that this renewal will be effected in a progressive and tentative manner something like the liturgical changes.

But whatever the manner of procedure there are certain norms which seem essential if the revised Code is to implement and continue the work of Vatican Council II.

The Canon Law Society of America is an organization with about twelve hundred members. In recent years this Society has sponsored various meetings, workshops and projects for the renewal of Church legislation.

Two years ago the national convention of the Society approved a series of resolutions for the renewal of Canon Law. It is the purpose of this paper to offer some brief reflections on these norms. First, the text of the document:

"The members of the Canon Law Society of America gathered in national assembly at their twenty-seventh convention are convinced that a substantial renewal of canon law will not be effected merely by changes in individual laws. What is required is a radical reappraisal of the rights and responsibilities of individuals and institutions in the modern world.

Therefore we resolve that the following recommendations be adopted as expressing norms considered necessary by the members of this Society, namely:

1. That there be a re-evaluation of the nature and purpose of the law in so far as it tends to perfect the people of God.

2. That in this re-evaluation cognizance be taken of the current scriptural and theological clarifications of the nature and mission of the Church.

3. That charity and pastoral concern be strong motivating factors in the formulation of the law, e.g., laws of burial, laws affecting non-Catholics, laws concerning annulments and dissolutions of marriages.

4. That in addition to the concepts of Roman Law, the concepts of Germanic, Anglo-American, and Oriental Law be considered in the formulation of the revised Code of Canon Law.

5. That there be a careful scrutiny of those laws which were formulated in the historical context of conflict with Jews, Protestants, Orthodox, and/or other religious or secular bodies in so far as these laws may lead to inferences of lack of justice and lack of charity.

6. That persons who were not baptized in the Catholic Church, or who were not converted to the Catholic faith, be exempt from purely ecclesiastical laws.

7. That the content and terminology of the law be formulated with the presumption that persons who are not Catholic are persons of integrity and good faith.

8. That the objections of non-Catholics to the laws of the Church be thoughtfully considered, inasmuch as these objections may point to the lack of justice, equity, or charity in the law.

9. That the penal laws be drastically curtailed and simplified and that their application, for the greater part, be

placed in the hands of the local ordinary or regional and national conferences of bishops.

10. That an accused person be not punished unless he is aware of the nature of the accusation, the identity of his accuser, and the evidence of the truth of the accusation, and he has adequate opportunity to defend himself.

11. That wherever possible decisions, permissions, and delegations, now reserved to the Holy See, be transferred to local ordinaries.

12. That the safeguarding of the rights of persons be on a par with the safeguarding of the dignity of sacraments.

13. That the rights and interests of priests and religious, other than pastors and superiors, be defined and safeguarded.

14. That very serious consideration be given to the fact that, under the present laws of procedure, persons seeking annulments or dissolutions of marriages often suffer a grave injustice, inasmuch as they are not given an adequate opportunity to vindicate their rights or to seek relief.

15. That the rights and interests of the laity be clearly defined and safeguarded.

16. That the freedom of conscience of the individual person be respected and safeguarded, e.g., laws concerning the prohibition and censure of books.

17. That the work and experience of the United Nations and the World Council of Churches be taken into consideration in the formation of the new law.

> Approved unanimously
> Canon Law Society of America
> Twenty-seventh annual convention, 1965."

The norms may be grouped under four headings. The first group would constitute the basic principles and includes the first three resolutions. A second series, norms 5 through 8, might be called ecumenical principles. Norms 4 and 17 urge consideration for other systems and experiences and may be called "catholic" or "pluralistic" principles. A final group comprising norms 9 through 16 could be roughly described as dealing with the rights and dignity of persons.

NATURE AND ROLE OF SACRED CANONS

Recent studies and statements, especially Vatican Council II, have done much to sharpen and deepen our understanding of the nature and mission of the Church. The Church is primarily a community, not an institution. Its nature is rightly grasped when it is viewed as the People of God, the sacrament of salvation.

1. As the community, so the law which emanates from that community. Church law must not merely be true to the nature of the People of God, but must be a resplendent expression of that reality. Canonical legislation should give form to the visible community, it ought to reflect the spirit of Christ in this historical situation. As well as revealing to all the mercy and wisdom of God, Canon Law should seek to create a climate in which each member can participate fully and freely in the community of salvation.

2. The Church must continually read the signs of the times and speak to men in the language of the times. To allow this response to the call of the Spirit, Church law must be open and flexible enough to adjust to rapidly changing cultural circumstances. As new situations develop they are to be studied in their relation to revealed principles and law must be constantly reborn from the insights achieved. As the Church is always in need of reform, so too the law must be continually reformed. The Council fathers have made this necessity clear in relation to such matters as liturgy and religious life. The necessity is no less urgent for Church law in general.

3. Pope Benedict XV made provision for a sort of continual updating of Canon Law, but it was never employed. Some system must be found to allow the ready adaptation of laws to the varying and changeable circumstances in an ever developing reality.

4. One way in which this may be achieved is by taking seriously the doctrine of the activity of the Holy Spirit in the People of God. Allowance must be made within the framework of Church laws for the Holy Spirit to speak forth. The guiding insights and salvific activity of the Spirit are present outside of the hierarchy as well as in the hierarchy. Could not the needs and desires of the local Church express themselves in customs?

5. The purpose of the law must be seen as primary and the letter merely as a means to the goal. Whenever the observance of a means hinders or endangers the attainment of the goal, the means should cease to be binding.

6. Where legislation does not truly reflect the mercy of Christ, it fails its purpose. Whenever, for example, a national conference of bishops could agree that a particular norm is useless, unreasonable or foolish for their country, it should be clear that such a norm fails to fulfill an essential requirement for Church regulations. Such a norm ceases to be a true law unless in a rare case the principle of solidarity might require its observance in one country for the good of the brothers in another country.

7. Pope Pius XII reaffirmed the principle that "the law is made for the people and not the people for the sake of the law".[1] Some restrictive legislation concerning burials hurts only the living and serves no proportionate good in our pluralistic society.

8. Is it not possible to consider the sacred canons as advisory guidelines rather than as binding legislation? This concept of binding legislation was introduced rather late in the life of the Church. Surely advisory guidelines from the salvation-community are as forceful as laws. In addition to attaining the goal in a more human manner, guidelines allow for more responsible variation in differing circumstances.

[1] PIUS XII, *A.A.S.*, Vol. 33, 421.

ECUMENICAL PRINCIPLES

Resolutions 5 through 8 treat of the law in its relationship with those who are not Catholic. It has frequently been observed that ecclesiastical practices and policies, the external forms and order of a Church, constitute a great hindrance when various Christians discuss union.[2] The more these differences can be overcome the easier it is for us to draw closer together. This is not to suggest that forms and practices should be uniform. Quite the contrary: a wide diversity of structure responding to the multiple needs of various mentalities and cultures will help much.

1. Would not a great diversity of means toward commonly accepted goals promote an ecumenical spirit?

2. Many Protestant theologians and some Roman Catholics question the concept of legal structures which "seriously bind the conscience". Would it not be useful to avoid confusion between ethical and legal areas?

3. Terminology which is common to the rest of the Christian community might well be adopted by Canon Law. It would seem that a genuine poverty of spirit might suggest this. Surely the term "Church Order" serves as well as "Canon Law". Nor would the terminology be that unusual for Roman Catholics since we frequently use it in reference to liturgical books and regulations.

4. Perhaps there could be a legal recognition of ecumenical fellowship, constituting juridic bodies to further this fellowship.

PLURALISTIC PRINCIPLES

We can benefit from the work and experience of other international institutions that deal with areas and interests quite similar to those of the Church.

Also there are other legal systems that ought to be studied.

[2] L. Vischer, *The Jurist*, Vol. 26 (1966) 395.

The Anglo-American tradition is the only legal structure that grew out of a Christian culture. Other systems current in the Christian world were inherited from a pagan society and modified by Christian principles.

A large segment of the Catholic and Christian world lives under the Anglo-American system and its thought patterns are native to them. Legal patterns based upon another system frequently offend their sense of values and impress them as harsh and even, at times, unjust. The same must be true of peoples accustomed to various other legal systems. But Church law ought to respect these values so highly prized by the men of our times.

Canon Law, as an absolute minimum, must manifest at least the same love for justice shown by civil law. It is a scandal when Church law does not demonstrate a respect for the dignity and integrity of the individual at least equal to that shown by the law of the land. Is it too much to hope that Church law outshine secular societies in its love for mercy, justice and freedom?

The principle of equity that has such a glorious heritage in Anglo-American law could well be incorporated into Canon Law. If the revised Code contained only a broad constitutional law to be implemented by national or regional structures and by-laws, then the legal system of each culture could be reflected in Church legislation.

RIGHTS OF PERSONS

In these norms we come to the area presenting some of the most poignant problems within the Church today. Our society has a large and growing class of efficient service personnel and managers. These men and women are keenly conscious of dealing with people in a proper and fitting manner, of respecting their rights and feelings. When Church administration does not display this same courteous regard, it is both a shock and a scandal.

In our educated world we have many people who are quite accustomed to make important decisions, to bear responsibility, to manifest initiative and creativity. At work they feel as an important part of the team and they strive to communicate this sense of belonging to those under them.

Yet our law regards all of these competent persons as though they were still simple and untrained people. We must create structures which give recognition to the insights of intelligent members of the community. Church law must have a profound regard for the psychological needs of a growing intellectual group in the assembly. This is particularly true in regard to the changed status of women in our society. Present legislation reflects the reality of the culture in which it was formulated, but it is glaringly out of harmony with the present realities. Perhaps nowhere is this more evident than in the case of women Religious. In general our current regulations lag far behind Catholic teaching on the rights and dignity of human beings.

1. Especially when law simply states what is already required by the nature of Christian life, it is better to appeal to man's nobler instincts and refrain from ordering him to these acts. It seems more Christian to appeal to an enlightened conscience than resort to an imperative.

2. There ought to be some clear definition of the rights and duties of persons, especially of those who share in the service of governing the Church. Only in this way can each man's freedom be assured.

3. Both the right of dissent and redress against the misuse of authority are essential if the dignity and freedom of individuals are to be safeguarded. Might it not be good to separate the administrative function from the judicial? On most levels an appeal against an administrative act is to the administrator himself.

4. Administrative ease and efficiency should never be preferred to the good of individuals. But all too frequently this is the case. A regulation is upheld as absolute even when, in an individual instance, it works a great harm.

5. Equal rights for men and women has been common coin-

age in the Western world for a generation. Pope John XXIII accepted the validity of the principle.[3] There was a day when women were neither able nor accustomed to handle financial affairs. Again there was a time when no decent woman ventured out of the house alone. It may be true today in certain circumstances. Mature women decide for themselves whether they need a companion and women Religious should be recognized as having equal maturity. Canonical enactments on financial matters, companion outside the house, special confessors and other details which presume immaturity should be changed.

6. Liturgical restrictions on women have been crumpling. Women are now permitted to sing in the choir. May they not be encouraged to take full and equal part in the worship of God? Should there be a universal prohibition against women coming into the sanctuary or reading the lessons at Mass? If there are cultures or countries where this may prove shocking the Conference of Bishops can provide.

These are but a few of the considerations that flow from the norms suggested by the Canon Law Society of America. Changes in individual laws are, indeed, required. But that is not enough. Church law must be clearly placed in a contemporary setting, presenting to all who read its ordinances and see its results a lovable, authentic expression of "the light of Christ brightly visible on the countenance of the Church".[4]

[3] *Pacem in Terris,* A.A.S., 55, 261 and 267.
[4] *Lumen Gentium,* n. 1.

Hubert Proesmans, C.SS.R./*Louvain, Belgium*

Religious Orders in the Pastoral Work of the Diocese and Parish

This subject is no longer new, although I doubt that that could have been said at the opening of Vatican Council II. However, from their beginning the religious orders have in one way or another played an active part in the diocesan apostolate.[1] But systematic theology, even the theology of the religious life,[2] has paid very little attention to this mission of the orders and congregations. The Code of Canon Law speaks of it so rarely that, in effect, it ignores it.[3]

On the other hand the publications of the Holy See, especially in recent decades, give us endless descriptions of the apostolate of the religious orders, their heroism, their field of action, and their methods.[4]

But it was not until Vatican Council II that the religious orders were given their definite place in the pastoral work of the diocese and the parish. First of all, the diocese itself had to be rethought in the light of the new emphasis on "decentralization",[5] which fixes the attention more on the local community

[1] Cf. R. Carpentier, *L'évêque et la vie consacrée, dans l'épiscopat et l'Église universelle* (Paris, 1962), p. 411.

[2] Cf. J. Suenens, *La Promotion apostolique de la religieuse* (Bruges, 1963).

[3] Cf. Canons 456, 608, 874, 1333, 1334, 1338, 1349, 1350, 1375.

[4] Cf. *Les Instituts de vie parfaite*, in the series "Les Enseignements Pontificaux," edited by the Monks of Solesmes (Tournai, 1962), pp. 59-63.

[5] Cf. E. Schillebeeckx, O.P., "Collaboration des religieux avec l'épiscopat," in *La vie consacrée* 38 (1966), n. 2.

and confronts the religious with the urgent work that needs to be done in the diocese and the parish. From now on, in all spheres, theological reflection will be striving to give us a program as well as a theory.[6]

I

PRELIMINARY PROGRAM

1. *An Attitude of Non-Engagement?*

The convent gives the impression of taking an attitude of non-engagement in the diocesan structure, and even more so in the parochial structure. Religious have special rights; they are often exempted from duties, have a tendency to introversion and are called to an eschatological state of life. In pastoral matters the particular apostolate of their institute is what primarily interests them. This conclusion seems clear and is supported by the facts: our monks and nuns find it difficult to engage in general pastoral work.

[6] *Ibid.,* pp. 75-90; O. Semmelroth, "Ecclesiologische Standortsbestimmung der Orden in Lichte des II. Vaticanischen Konzils," in *Ordenskorrespondenz* (1966), p. 351; S. Klocknes, O.F.M., "Seelsorge in und mit der Diözese," in *Ordenskorrespondenz* (1966), pp. 374-85; F. Wulf, "Hierarchie und Orden," in *Ordenskorrespondenz* (1964); A. Scheuermann, "Die rechtlichen Beziehungen zwischen Orden und Hierarchie in heutiger Sicht," in *Ordenskorrespondenz* (1964); P. Regamey, "La consécration religieuse," in *La vie consacrée* (1966), pp. 266-94, 339-59; J. Hamer, *Place des religieux dans l'apostolat* (Paris, 1964), pp. 97-114; J. Urtasin, "L'évêque et les religieux," *ibid.,* pp. 115-21. S. Kleiner, "L'exemption vue par les religieux," *ibid.,* pp. 123-33; L. Moreels, S.J., "Diocesane congregatie en einheidspastoraal," in *De Klosterling* (1965), pp. 75-83; P. Martelet, S.J., "Le rôle charismatique de toute vie religieuse dans l'Eglise," in *Assemblées Générales union des superieures majeures des instituts feminins de Belgique* (1966), pp. 109-118; J. Beyer, S.J., "La Consécration religieuse dans le mystere de l'Eglise," *ibid.,* pp. 81-108; A. Renard, *Vie apostolique de la religieuse d'aujourd'hui* (Bruges, 1962); W. Sternemann, "Das Seelsorgeamt als Kontaktstelle zwischen Bischof und Orden," *ibid.,* pp. 40-2; L. Bosse, "Aussergewöhnliche Seelsorge in der pastoralen Plan," *ibid.,* pp. 42-7; E. Colomb, "Dienst der Orden in einer veränderten Seelsorgestruktur," *ibid.,* pp. 48-52; H. Patt, "Die Aufgaben der Ordenskleur in der neuen Situation der Kirche," *ibid.,* pp. 151-60; P. Israel, "Ordensgemeinschaften und Diözesen nach dem II. Vaticanischen Konzil," in *Ordenskorrespondenz* (1967), pp. 1-10; P. Hofmeister, "Die Exemption der Ordensgenossenschaften," *ibid.,* pp. 11-25.

When we examine the state of affairs more closely, there is no doubt at all that the position of religious is not "structural". "In the care of souls . . . they do not occupy the most important position in the individual Church." [7] But by reason of their state they are bound to live intensely the mystery of the Church universal, and they see themselves as part of the People of God scattered throughout the earth. At this level they have a special vocation in the diocese and the parish. Vatican Council II proclaimed that the bishop is a "member of the college of bishops . . . which exists for the sake of the universal Church",[8] and in particular for the missions;[9] that in the individual Church the Church of Christ is truly active, the one, holy, catholic and apostolic Church;[10] that every priest is first of all a priest of the universal Church[11] by virtue of his grace for the good of the whole Church.[12] It is the function of monasteries and convents to remind us, by their organization and the very structure of their vocation, of the need to be open to the whole Church and of the presence of catholicity at the diocesan level. Let us not be too quick to say that religious are disengaged from the local community. Even here we find they have "another" commitment distinct from the diocesan apostolate. To reduce all commitments to the same level and to require uniformity would be to the detriment of the local as well as the universal Church.

2. Co-workers with the Bishop by Their State of Life

Our starting point must be the participation of all in the mystery of the Church. Bishops and religious are first of all members of the People of God, "whose head is Christ, and who seek order and freedom, law and love, the purpose and the glory of God".[13] They are in the communion of faith, love and prayer;

[7] Decree *Christus Dominus*, n. 28.
[8] Constitution *Lumen Gentium*, n. 23; Decree *Christus Dominus*, nn. 3 and 4.
[9] Decree *Christus Dominus*, nn. 6 and 7.
[10] *Ibid.*, n. 11.
[11] Constitution *Lumen Gentium*, n. 28; Decree *Christus Dominus*, n. 34.
[12] Constitution *Lumen Gentium*, n. 28.
[13] P. Martelet, *op. cit.*, p. 111.

they share the same hope, the same baptism, and they celebrate the same eucharist. They are confronted with the same mysteries of life and have heard the same call to work for the salvation of the world. The apostolic community begins at the level of this fullness of life.

The functions differ, but they are in the service of the same call. "The first of the chief functions of the bishop," [14] "his most important commission," [15] is to preach the Gospel. To carry weight, this preaching must have experience behind it—the bishop's own, of course—the experience of the whole Church, but particularly the experience of a consecrated life. "The profession of the evangelical counsels is a sign to attract all the members of the Church; it shows forth visibly in this world the presence of heavenly blessings and bears witness to the new life. . . . It announces the resurrection . . . and manifests the kingdom of God. . . ." [16] Second, the bishop has a "commission to sanctify". [17] By being themselves masters of perfection, bishops "will induce their priests, religious and laity to progress in holiness, each according to his calling".[18] If the call to holiness is addressed to all the baptized without reservation,[19] religious in particular will seek an evangelical state of life which will give them special means of "attaining the perfection of charity, in action".[20]

Finally, the episcopacy belongs to the structure of the Church; it is of sacramental origin. If it "rules by counsel, persuasions and example, it has also the authority and the sacred power to edify".[21] Religious do not have a special place in this structure;[22] they are a charismatic sector of the Church by virtue of their

[14] Constitution *Lumen Gentium*, n. 25.
[15] Decree *Christus Dominus*, n. 12.
[16] Constitution *Lumen Gentium*, n. 44.
[17] Decree *Christus Dominus*, n. 15.
[18] *Ibid.*
[19] Constitution *Lumen Gentium*, n. 40.
[20] *S. Th.*, IIa, IIae, q. 44, a. 4 ad 3.
[21] Decree *Perfectae caritatis*, n. 2.
[22] Decree *Christus Dominus*, n. 35; n. 28 of the Motu Propio *Ecclesiae Sanctae* is an exception here.

individual charism as well as their collective inspiration. Charismatics need episcopal authority, and not only to receive once and for all their guarantee of authenticity, but also to live and develop with ecclesiastical authority where they are called to work. On their part, these charismatics can, in freedom of spirit, counteract the danger of hardening which threatens all structures and administrations.

Thus even if one only considers the presence of religious in the diocese or parish at the level of their life in communion with the individual Church and insofar as this communion actually exists, we already find a real and effective cooperation.

In fact this is not always the case. Many convents are too closed in and do not have a concrete share in the Christian life of the diocese or parish. They have Christian life inside their buildings; outside it is mission. Of course they need an intimate family life, belonging to the community alone. This is legitimately reserved for religious. But the mysteries of Christian life should be celebrated together with the outside community. In the future there should be a more pronounced effort to cooperate at the diocesan and parochial level, the better to express the unity of the Christian mystery.

II

THE PASTORAL COMMISSION

The preceding section suggested the basis of a sincere understanding in the pastoral field. So far the principles and the situation have been fairly clear. But in considering the cooperation of seculars and regulars at the level of actual pastoral activity, difficulties arise.

The coordination of the various elements is not easy; these elements include structures and charismata, the needs of the local Church and the special apostolate of the religious Order, the authority of the bishop and the authority of the religious superior, the personality of the bishop and his "secular" helpers, and the personality of the religious superior and the members of his Order. The concrete situation with which we are familiar and the norms which have just been laid down by Rome both teach us that the tensions in this area are sometimes very severe.

We should bear in mind that the existence of the tension is a normal state of affairs, but it should not lead to a stagnant hostility which might be a scandal to the People of God. On the contrary this tension should be beneficial and enriching. As we have already suggested, the structures should make the charismata efficient and define their functions; the charismata in turn should act to prevent the hardening of the structures; the special apostolate of the Order should consider the needs of the local Church and the horizons of the local Church should be widened by the special apostolate of the Order; the bishop should dispose of his resources according to the needs of his Church; the religious superior, while remaining faithful to the spirit of his Order and taking into account the resources available to him, will help the needs of the universal Church; the various authorities will recognize the necessity of regulations, but they will avoid all hardening and adopt the noble attitude inspired by true charity.

But we should add that these principles of mutual understanding do not touch upon the problem of cooperation in the various kinds of mission. We shall try to throw a little light on this subject by distinguishing the ordinary case, where the special apostolate of the Order easily finds its place in the general pastoral work of the diocese, and certain other more complicated situations.

1. *The Special Apostolate of the Order*

If we are permitted to proceed by enunciating propositions, we should enunciate the following as our first: "When a bishop calls religious, this is a continuation of the call of his predecessors. He asks them first of all to exercise in his diocese the apostolic charism proper to their Order for the good of the people entrusted to his care."

It seems that there is still a certain uneasiness even in the documents of Vatican Council II and the most recent pronouncements of the Holy See. As a general rule the documents concerned with the religious life insist on fidelity to the fundamental inspiration and special apostolate of the Order; they go on to speak of the need to adapt these to the conditions existing at different times and places.[23] The documents concerned with the episcopacy state it otherwise: the bishop, according to the needs of his Church, can ask for help from religious, while respecting their constitutions and their special apostolate.[24] The perspective is different, in theory and in practice, and reconciliation is difficult. We think the apostolic charism and the original inspiration of the Order should be regarded as of first importance, for this charism is the best help the religious can offer the local Church. The bishop cannot do better than preserve this charism as far as he possibly can. This is not difficult to prove. When a bishop invites a modern foundation into his diocese, such as the Brothers of the Virgin of the Poor, the Apostolic Institute of the Workers' Mission of SS. Peter and Paul, or the Brothers or Sisters of Charles de Foucauld, he does so with the intention of having for his diocese not just general helpers who are perhaps necessary for the good of this local Church, but helpers with the particular apostolic charism of their Order. Applying the same norm to older foundations is perhaps more dubious. But nevertheless the bishops in council prescribed fidelity to the spirit of the founder and the intensification of its apostolate by a realization of the aims of the Order. It is therefore logical that the bishop should make use of the religious of his diocese, not simply in general apostolic work according to the urgent needs of his Church, but first and foremost that they may exercise in his territory the function belonging to their Order. This function, except in exceptional circumstances which we will discuss further on, is a response to a spiritual need of his Church.

While bearing this in mind, we may expect that cooperation

[23] Cf. E. Schillebeeckx, *op. cit.*, p. 80; J. Hamer, *op. cit.*, pp. 111-2.
[24] I, nn. 28 and 29.

in general pastoral work will normally come quite naturally, even though fairly complicated prescriptions may be canonically necessary. The Motu Proprio *Ecclesiae sanctae* makes this clear.

2. *Special Apostolate and Special Circumstances*

The ideal coordination which we have just suggested does not exist. In actual fact, it is necessary to take into account the situation of the diocese, the Orders and the persons involved. It is therefore necessary to adjust the general rule to the existing facts. The Council and the post-conciliar commissions will give us directives. It is possible that certain apostolic charismata are no longer fulfilling the function they were intended to fulfill and that new and more urgent work is being neglected for lack of workers.

Coordination in these cases may be obtained in various ways:

(a) if possible, by the adaptation of the Order to this state of affairs;[25]

(b) by allowing temporarily, or for certain members of the Order, an exception to its rule (particularly in regard to the organization of parishes);

(c) by moving, if an Order in a particular diocese or parish no longer finds a suitable field of action. Mobility is proper to religious and this is perhaps too often forgotten. But real prudence is necessary in this situation; the Order should be courageous enough to make the move if necessary, but should not forget the apostolic advantages of stability.[26]

The option of an apostolate other than that intended at the foundation of the Order may be justifiable for the whole Order or for certain of its members. An Order may have good workers but still feel itself incapable of change and renewal; it then could affiliate with an Order of the same family or attempt a total reconstruction.[27]

---

[25] Decree *Christus Dominus*, n. 35.

[26] Motu Proprio *Ecclesiae sanctae*, n. 34.

[27] Decree *Perfectae caritatis*, n. 21; Motu Proprio *Ecclesiae sanctae*, nn. 39-41; this solution is not explicitly mentioned in the documents quoted but it is being tried out in certain dioceses.

In every Order or Congregation there are members who, for one reason or another—sometimes special talents or a particular kind of spirituality—are clearly better off exercising an apostolate fairly different from that special to their Order. In these cases it is necessary to help the brother or sister to become better integrated into a new apostolic structure of the Church.

III

CONCLUSION

From a study of the recent documents of the Church, it appears that the place of the religious in the general apostolate is codified in accordance with certain guiding principles:

1. The bishop is in charge of coordinating the apostolate at the diocesan level.

2. It is necessary to make the best possible arrangement between the needs of the diocese and the special apostolate of the Order.

3. In order to obtain an arrangement which suits both parties, each must loyally fulfill its own obligations. If it is an apostolate with close local links to the activity of the convent, the religious superior must take chief responsibility; in all other cases the bishop's responsibility is more direct and important.

4. To avoid disagreements, written contracts should be drawn up whenever this appears necessary to the common enterprise.

5. A rule of conduct should be supplied to resolve the difficulties of the religious engaged in the apostolate.

6. The Church wants the religious, whatever the work he is doing, to exercise his apostolate *as* a true religious.[28]

Successful cooperation will not be possible, whatever prescriptions are made, if the persons involved do not share the spirit of the Church and true Christian charity. These two necessities must

[28] J. Pfab, "Der Bischof als erster Seelsorger," in *Paulus* (1966), pp. 33-9; Decree *Christus Dominus,* n. 35; Motu Proprio *Ecclesiae sanctae,* nn. 22-40.

be repeatedly stressed. This successful cooperation can take place in the formal "collaboration of the councils of major superiors and episcopal conferences",[29] in the "council of the presbytery"[30] and the "pastoral council".[31] At these regular meetings people should learn how to work together. If the gathering is truly representative, if it takes place with the sign of faith, and with confidence in the work to be done and in openness of spirit for new initiatives, the future will be full of promise.

[29] Decree *Perfectae caritatis,* n. 23.
[30] Motu Proprio, *Ecclesiae sanctae,* n. 15.
[31] *Ibid.,* n. 16.

Charles Munier / *Strasbourg, France*

Episcopal Conferences

Chapter 3 of the conciliar decree *Christus Dominus,* promulgated on October 28, 1965, treats the problems connected with episcopal cooperation for the common good of several Churches. Having expressed the desire that "the venerable institution of synods and councils flourish with new vigor", it defines the concept, the structures and the competence of episcopal conferences (n. 38); it had already stressed their importance and their apostolic benefits (n. 37). The following year, the Motu proprio *Ecclesiae sanctae* (August 6, 1966) spelled out the ways in which the conciliar decree could be implemented as far as episcopal conferences are concerned (n. 41).

Essential to the life of the Church, synodal activity finds its most solemn expression in an ecumenical council. It is nevertheless necessary on lower levels, as a symbol of communion, in faith and charity, among Churches that participate, and as an instrument of their planned and coordinated pastoral activity.

Symbol of Communion

The first aspect opens out in the conciliar liturgy, which is thoroughly suffused with the presence of Christ (Mt. 18, 20) and the Holy Spirit. The *Ordines de celebrando concilio,* whose essential features were defined at the 4th Council of Toledo

(633), have transmitted to us the beautiful prayer *Adsumus Domine Sancte Spiritus,* which is still in use. The national Visigoth councils consecrated three days (*die litaniarum*) to fasting and to meditation on the Creed. An ancient custom, attested to by the Councils of Nicea, Constantinople (381) and Chalcedon, chose to have questions relating to faith examined before any others. Although the liturgy for episcopal conferences has taken on new shape in our day, it is still inscribed in this tradition and remains a suppliant petition, a living demonstration of faith and charity.

Instrumental Role

The instrumental role of episcopal conferences is too obvious to require stressing here. The Council calls upon them to become the privileged organism of union, coordination and mutual collaboration between bishops; to resolve to work for the common good of their Churches, and to participate generously in the concern of the Roman pontiff for all the Churches.

An episcopal conference is only a new form of local synods, whose origins date back to the first centuries of Christianity and whose changing fortunes have been depicted many times. It is worth noting that all the various reform movements, whether stimulated by local initiative or directed by Rome, strove to restore new life to this institution. We need only recall the efforts of St. Boniface (8th century) and Hincmar of Rheims (9th century), or the initiatives of the Gregorian era. Lateran IV (1215) assigned to provincial councils the task of ensuring the execution of the norms of common law, and it prescribed an annual meeting for them. The Council of Trent (Session XXIV, c.2 De ref.) wanted them every three years; Pope Sixtus V provided for review of their decrees by the Sacred Congregation of the Council before their promulgation (Bull, *Immensa aeterni,* 1587).

During the course of the last four centuries, political circumstances and many other centrifugal tendencies have not favored the institution of local, provincial or national councils. It is understandable that, in countries where Christianity was newly established, Rome would want to exercise strict control over all forms of synodal activity—directing their plenary councils, over which Rome's legates presided, and subjecting the decisions of these councils to her *recognitio* (Can. 291, §1). The Code of Canon Law retained these diverse forms of conciliar life which, to be sure, had been greatly weakened by Roman centralization and lethargic on the local level. Thus, for example, provincial synods were only obliged to meet every five years; this prevented them from having any continuing impact that was truly in line with the real dimensions of their pastoral problems (Can. 283-86). National councils did not have any legal existence; plenary councils, which took their place in some areas, were organized in such a way that they could be kept under strict control (Can. 281-82). Episcopal meetings, set for every five years, found their action limited to the preparation of provincial councils, spaced far apart and deprived of any real authority (Can. 292).

Yet, the latter gave rise to the present episcopal conferences, which Vatican Council II has blessed and for which it has set down the proper forms of their normative activity.[1]

It is evident that the term covers quite different realities (in number of members, frequency of meetings, work procedures, chief organisms, etc.). That is why the Motu proprio *Ecclesiae sanctae* does more than urge bishops, in nations or territories where episcopal conferences do not yet exist, to establish them as soon as possible and to draw up statutes for the Holy See's examination (n. 41, §1). It also demands that established episcopal conferences frame their statutes according to the prescriptions of the Council; and if they have already formulated them, they are to be revised according to the spirit of the Council and then sent to Rome for examination (§2).

Even when they are created to respond to practical needs,

[1] The *Annuario Pontificio* (1967) mentions the existence of 61 episcopal conferences. 30 of them have statutes approved *ad experimentum* between 1955 and 1967, and 2 of them have statutes approved *ad quinquennium* (Australia and Madagascar). 9 others have had their statutes approved simply or definitively between 1882 (Ireland) and 1962 (Japan).

ecclesiastical structures reflect the Church's awareness of itself. Episcopal conferences do not merely represent the bishops' new-found awareness of their common responsibilities, whose urgency and seriousness are clearly evident; in the institutional sphere, they embody the doctrinal reflection that has taken place with regard to collegiality. Cardinal Doepfner, a member of the Council's Coordinating Commission, asked the responsible commission to point up clearly the link between episcopal conferences and the theological principle of collegiality. The same request was made by several speakers during the conciliar debates, but some eminent opponents denied this connection or searched for some substitute principle of a more general nature, e.g., the principle of communion between local Churches, of the spiritual mission of bishops, or of the needs of the missions. The Decree *Christus Dominus* avoided making any pronouncement on this fundamental problem. Neither did it try to abolish the traditional system of the Oriental Churches; but it did encourage the institution of synods within the framework of patriarchates (n. 38, §6).

Some Council fathers were afraid that episcopal conferences would bring back the specter of national Churches or of secret oligarchies manipulating the organisms of the secretariats and commissions. In spite of their fears Vatican Council II was not afraid to grant episcopal conferences real legislative power, which is to be exercised according to the norms of the decree (n. 38, §4).

Juridically binding decisions (cases prescribed by common law or covered by a special mandate from the Holy See, on its own initiative or at the demand of the conference) shall hereafter require a two-thirds majority of those members eligible to vote (whether they are present or not). Moreover, before being promulgated, these decisions must be "recognized" by the Holy See. For other decisions (without binding juridical force), the episcopal conference itself is free to determine the conditions surrounding them; that is, the majority required, how they are to be promulgated and implemented, etc.

Taking part in the activities of the episcopal conferences, but exercising different degrees of competence, are all local ordinaries of any and every rite (but not vicars general), coadjutors, auxiliary bishops and other titular bishops who exercise a particular charge with regard to the general pastoral welfare (not the diocesan). Other titular bishops are not *de jure* members of the episcopal conference, nor are the legates of the Roman pontiff (n. 38, §2).

The decree then spells out the degrees of competence. Local ordinaries and coadjutors have a deliberative vote; auxiliary bishops and other *de jure* members will have a deliberative or a consultative vote, depending on the statutes of the conference. Considering the pastoral responsibilities that they assume, it is probable that auxiliary bishops will get a deliberative vote. Resigned or retired bishops will probably retain a consultative vote. It is worth noting that the decree makes no mention of religious superiors; yet it seems that their presence at episcopal conferences could be quite useful, indeed sometimes necessary.

Work Procedures

The most thoroughly organized episcopal conferences already in existence have adopted organisms and work procedures that have been tested for several decades in many areas where collective or collegial work plays a role, e.g., those to be found in specialized types of Catholic Action (General Assembly, Permanent Council, Commissions, etc.).

It is in the plenary assembly, its essential organism, that the episcopal conference expresses its new awareness of apostolic problems and its desire to deal with them by concerted action (employing binding juridic force, if necessary). It goes without saying that the relevance of this action will depend, first of all, on having up-to-date information. This will be provided by the service bureaus entrusted with the task of preparing the work of the Assembly. The decree allows great latitude to the conferences in determining what organisms are indispensable for their effective operation. But it does suggest that the conference have a Permanent Council, Episcopal Commissions, and a General Secretariat (n. 38, §3).

After the statutes of various episcopal conferences have been duly approved by the Holy See and promulgated, it will be possible to compare their various work procedures and the instruments of coordination, information and implementation that they have adopted. From this standpoint, the conferences are at different stages in different countries. In some, the already existing structures integrate themselves very readily into the framework traced by the Council. In others, more or less thoroughgoing adaptations are required. And in still others, the many and varied problems faced by bishops are examined and straightened out at their regular meetings (monthly or whatever), there being no formal body of statutes.

As far as missionary countries are concerned, the conciliar decree *Ad gentes,* promulgated December 7, 1965, urged their episcopal conferences to "consider in common consultation the more serious questions and urgent problems", and "to join forces in setting up projects which serve the common good" lest "an insufficient supply of workers and resources be dissipated, or projects multiplied without need" (n. 31).

These recommendations also deal with the permanent apparatus ordinarily attached to episcopal conferences. Based on the example of CELAM, the general conference of the Latin American episcopate, pastoral and missionary cooperation seems likely to be more fruitful on a supra-national level. The Motu proprio *Ecclesiae sanctae* appears to favor such organizations; it stipulates that the Holy See must give them approval and draw up their statutes (n. 41, §§3, 4).

The organizational perfection of institutions is only one of the conditions that provide for their effective operation. So long as they remain connected to the vital impulse that gave rise to them, they will be able to exercise a vital function and overcome difficulties. But vital balance is a fragile plant, threatened by cancerous growths and local weeds. The history of the Church contains accounts of changing rhythms and loss of balance. The regulatory functions of the center do not always find the adhesion and the collaboration they desire; the center, on the other hand, can lose the proper tone and rhythm. Applied to episcopal conferences, these observations point out the importance of active participation by all their members, of a generous acceptance of one's proper responsibilities. The fruits will accrue only if the interest of the participants is constantly sustained, only if the work remains realistic and well organized.

Collegial Effort

Concretely, the members of episcopal conferences will demonstrate their desire to work together for the common good of their Churches by accepting an assignment in some commission, bureau, or committee. In reality, collegial activity is exercised at every level of the conference, not just at the top level—the plenary assembly. While the latter remains the clearest expression of collegial action, the organisms that prepare or carry out the decisions of the plenary assembly participate equally in the collegial power of the episcopal conference, which entrusts them with their particular mission and delegates the required authority to them.

We do not intend to give a detailed presentation of the machinery that will insure the sound functioning of an episcopal conference—by proper division of work and by clear-cut delegation of competence and authority. Episcopal conferences (whose statutes have already been published) have organized from 10 to 15 special commissions, plus a good half dozen committees and as many national secretariats. Obviously every sector of pastoral life and every institution of a general nature where the hierarchy exercises some measure of responsibility would seem to suggest the establishment of a competent organism. But the important point is that all forms of juridically organized collaboration express the collegial power of the episcopal conference.

This power is not the sum total of the powers of member bishops, nor is it a power delegated by the Holy See. It is a collegial power, an ordinary power properly exercised on this level

by the bishops, in union with the sovereign pontiff, and acknowl-
edged by him (through the promulgation of *Christus Dominus*
and through the *recognitio* that will be given to the conference's
decisions).

While one may be inclined to devote special attention to certain juridical aspects of episcopal conferences—because of their
newness on the institutional level—one should not forget the
wise remark of Cardinal Frings in this regard: "What counts in
these assemblies is not their juridical status, but the spirit of
freedom, of voluntary commitment and of fraternal charity."
The juridical elements are only instruments meant to serve the
pastoral mission of the Church. Episcopal conferences, whatever
forms they may take, have no other purpose.

John Oesterreicher/*South Orange, New Jersey*

Jewish Comments on the Conciliar Statement about the Jews

"May he who blessed our fathers
Abraham, Isaac, and Jacob,
Moses and Aaron, David and
Solomon, the prophets of Israel, and all the just ones of the
world bless the pope and send blessing and prosperity on all the
works of his hands."

This was the Sabbath prayer of a 15th-century Jewish community of southern France for the pope of its day: it was divulged by the American Rabbi Marc Tanenbaum and applied to Pope John, at the time of the opening of the Ecumenical Council. Publication of the prayer was as much an affectionate testimonial to the pope as it was an expression of Jewish hopes.[1]

Affirmation and Hope

Rabbi Tanenbaum is Director of the Interreligious Affairs Department of the American Jewish Committee. His counterparts in another Jewish organization, the Anti-Defamation League of B'nai B'rith, are Dr. Joseph Lichten and Rabbi Arthur Gilbert. In an address delivered at a Catholic college in March, 1964, Dr. Lichten, too, hailed the spirit of Pope John:

"The atmosphere the late supreme pontiff created, in keeping

[1] *New York Herald-Tribune*, 10/14/1962.

97

with his policy of aggiornamento or contemporaneousness for the Church, did much to change and even reverse centuries-old hostilities between Catholics—I should say Christians—and non-Christians. His peculiar genius for brotherliness toward those not of his own Catholic family inspired in Jews a reciprocal optimism that I would call unprecedented in our two millennia of common history."

Dr. Lichten traced "the deep [interest of Jews] in the Council's deliberations" to their long history of pain: "Much of the impact of the draft statement on Catholic-Jewish relations is attributable to the fact that none of us is able to forget the recent world disaster which brought death to 6 million innocent Jewish victims. Anti-Semitism has existed for centuries, to be sure, but 'the final solution', the diabolic Nazi plan to exterminate the people of Israel *in toto,* originated in *this* century." [2]

Two months earlier, Rabbi Gilbert compared the attitude of Vatican Council II with Vatican Council I which had before it a plan to invite the conversion of Jews. Jews, he held, would have "resented and rejected" such an invitation. Turning to Vatican Council II, he exclaimed: "There is no more talking down to the Jews; no more of the stereotypic conception of the Jew. . . . The 'experts' assigned today to the Church Secretariat concerned with this project [do not act] in a condescending way. They are responsive to our concerns and speak for us. . . . This [is] the glory of [the Council's] proposal. Catholics, although holding to a conviction in the truth of their faith and to the dream of a reunion of all into their Church, declare nevertheless: we have a responsibility to achieve mutual esteem and understanding through discussion, and study, through knowing who you are and trying to understand what you believe. No matter what our differences, we are obliged to condemn any act that will harm you. . . . It seems to me when I hear this that all we—in the Jewish community—can do is to say *ken yehi ratzon,* 'may the Lord make it so'." [3]

[2] From a lecture, as printed by *The Catholic Messenger,* 4/2/64.
[3] *The Reconstructionist,* 1/10/64, pp. 8-9.

Dismay and Strictures

Though no Jew can speak for the entire American Jewish community, much less the world Jewish community, the three reactions just given to the draft of 1964 bespeak a broad consensus. But as soon as the final version became known, the tone of the response changed. Enthusiasm gave way to widespread dismay, praise to stricture. The often hostile criticism was occasioned by the changes made in the final document, though frequently not by the changes themselves, rather as the newspapers magnified and overplayed them. Out of such an atmosphere one could often hear the summary statement: "Too little, too late." A writer for the *Jerusalem Post* even held that the conciliar statement "had come about 1,500 years—or at least 25 years—too late".[4] Such sullenness is frightening; one fears for, and sympathizes with, its victim.

An editorial in the *Cleveland Jewish News* read: "The declaration no longer asserts—as approved in draft form last year—that 'the Jewish people should never be presented as one rejected, cursed or guilty of deicide'. [To be exact, only the words 'guilty of deicide' disappeared from the final text.] Does the anti-Semite need more than this widely publicized deletion to confirm him in his anti-Semitism—to maintain and insist that the charge of deicide may properly be made against the Jewish people?"[5] One may regret the deletion—I do so most keenly—and still understand why some thought it necessary. One may grieve at the change and yet ask the editorialist if he really believes that an anti-Semitic diehard needs to be confirmed in his aberration? Incidentally, whose fault is it that the deletion was widely publicized and, what is worse, wrongly interpreted?

So highly charged was the reaction that Rabbi Abraham Joshua Heschel—widely acclaimed as a sage—declared: "Not to condemn the demonic canard of deicide, a cause of murder and pogroms, would mean condoning Auschwitz, defiance of the God

---

[4] *Jerusalem Post Weekly*, 12/10/65.
[5] *The Cleveland Jewish News*, 10/22/67.

of Abraham and an act of paying homage to Satan." [6] This is an accusation so wild that silence is the best answer.

Jewish critics claimed more than once that it had taken the Council years to come up with a declaration from which all warmth was gone; they complained that it was discussed at length, that one version followed upon another—all of which proved to them that the Church did not really mean what she said; that the statement did not come from the heart.[7] It never occurred to these precipitous critics that a document of great consequences called for a thoroughgoing discussion. That the champions of the Declaration never tired of arguing against a vociferous minority betrays a deep commitment, not lack of interest.

A Case of Gall and Vinegar

One of the most ill-tempered reactions was that of Rabbi Eisendrath. In his 1965 presidential message to the General Assembly of the Union of American Hebrew Congregations, he confessed to frustration at seeing the final document "substantially diluted". He readily adopted the outrageous accusation by *The Christian Century* I already quoted in *Concilium* (Vol. 24, p. 151) in which the editors accused the Council of "monstrous arrogance", of "a crime against the Jews", of "a sin against God", because the bishops assumed the "power to forgive or not forgive Jews for a crime of which [the Jews] are not guilty".

Nowhere in the Council's statement on the Jews is it stated or implied that they are now "absolved". The notion is derived from newspaper headlines. To judge the Declaration on the basis of provocative captions rather than on its actual wording is bad. Rabbi Eisendrath went still further: he thought that the deficiencies he found in the document entitled him to put priests on notice: "Though hopeful that even the weakened Schema on the Jews may warn many a parish priest of the sinfulness of anti-Semitism, for synagogues scrawled with the crooked cross of the

---

[6] *Jewish Chronicle*, 10/8/65.
[7] See, for instance, Rabbi Dr. Naphtali Carlebach in *Aufbau*, 11/5/65.

swastika, for Jewish cemeteries desecrated, for discrimination and even of persecution yet manifesting itself in Europe, in South America and even in some parts of our own country . . . we must hold responsible still those who utter such inflammatory phrases as did Pope Paul when, in his Lenten Day [sic] sermon of April 4 last, he lashed his hearers into habitual Holy Week fanaticism by reminding them that the Jew, 'predestined to receive the Messiah, not only does not recognize him, but fights him, slanders him and finally kills him'." [8]

Pope Paul's sermon of Passion Sunday, 1965, was hardly inflammatory, and he certainly did not lash "his hearers into habitual Holy Week fanaticism." I do not scruple to say that his words were unfortunate. Still, like any other man, he has a right to be understood in context. The thrust of his sermon was toward the many who today oppose God. His reference to the clash between Jesus and "the Jewish people" was couched—alas!—in preconciliar language, yet it was no more than a rhetorical device seeking to provide a background for his complaint about the negative attitude of many moderns toward Christ.

Rabbi Eisendrath's feverish remarks stand in direct opposition to another of his messages—the one of November 16, 1963. In it, he "rejoiced in the forthright efforts of the Catholic Church . . . to advance the ecumenicity of Christendom. . . . The mind is staggered and the heart is enkindled by the prospect of a conciliar document that would lead, not only to a repudiation of anti-Semitism but also to a positive Christian thrust against it" and the enormous effects such a thrust would have on Jewish life everywhere.

Having thus eulogized the work of the Church, he went on to ask some embarrassing questions of his own community, in the belief that interreligious understanding cannot be a one-way street. "What about our Jewish attitude toward Christendom, toward Jesus especially? Are we to remain adamant . . . in our refusal to examine our own statements . . . our own inter-

[8] "The State of Our Union," 48th General Assembly, Union of American Hebrew Congregations, San Francisco, California, 11/14/65.

pretations of the significance of the life of Jesus, the Jew? Have
we examined our own books, official and otherwise, to re-
appraise our ofttimes jaundiced view of him in whose name
Christianity was established?" His questions became even more
painful: "How long shall we continue pompously to aver that
the chief contribution of Jesus was simply a rehash of all that
had been said before by his Jewish ancestors? How long before
we can admit that his influence was a beneficial one—not only
to the pagans but to the Jews of his time as well, and that only
those who later took his name in vain profaned his teaching?" [9]

Rabbi Eisendrath's probings were widely reported and almost
as widely opposed. He was treated, to use his own words, "to a
vicious attack from one of the leaders" of Reform Judaism.
Though unexpected, it was no new experience, for back in 1934
because of a similar stand, Rabbi Eisendrath was described "in
the lush and expressive language of the Yiddish press . . . as
a *mamzer* (bastard) and a *mashummed* (apostate)". In 1963,
his appeal for an unprejudiced appraisal of Jesus' "lofty and yet
so simply stated prophetic and rabbinic teachings" was greeted
"with an almost wholly visceral and vehement rejection".[10]
Understandably, the Rabbi was deeply wounded by the bitter
misinterpretations of his intent, and it looks as if his attacks on
the Council were a perhaps unconscious endeavor to repair his
assaulted honor and to regain the respect of his colleagues and
Jews in general. If this analysis is correct, one must ask whether
even so legitimate a desire as that of being understood may be
attained at the price of an unjust charge and of thus endangering
the not yet won but happily envisaged brotherhood of Christians
and Jews, a goal I assume dear to Rabbi Eisendrath.

More Bitterness

Among other bitter attacks is an editorial in *The Reconstructionist*. Its writer was upset because the final version did not

[9] Message of the President, Union of American Hebrew Congregations,
November 16, 1963.
[10] "The Case for Jesus' Rehabilitation," *The Jewish World,* December
1964, pp. 24-27.

explicitly reject the "charge of deicide" (which the author wrongly considered "the term traditionally used by the Church" for the condemnation and execution of Jesus), also because the Declaration only "deplored" hatred (which he understood only in its English meaning of mere regret, but not in the Latin significance of loud, vehement lamentation). Thus he writes: "One wonders, in the light of this statement, whether the Church will ever succeed in reforming itself unless it comes to grips with the cruel, even barbaric, aspects of its own history of literature; unless it reckons with its own past, acknowledges its own sins and repudiates them in the sight and hearing of all men." [11]

Another example of acrimony is "An Open Letter to the Pope" by Rabbi Julius J. Nodel of St. Louis on the occasion of the pope's visit to the United Nations. He accused the pope of "aggrandizing [his] own Church" because he—the guest of the United Nations—did not invite other religious leaders to plead the peace cause with him. Again and again, he linked Pope Paul's appearance at the United Nations disparagingly with the Council. To quote only one passage: "The Vatican Council has found various evasive doctrinal formulations, but in all of them the Jew remains the killer of God. You are trying to give evidence of your new won tolerance by making strenuous efforts to push the Jewish crime into the background of antiquity. You mean to be magnanimous and subtle, but we Jews feel like the innocent who has been forgiven a crime he never committed, and we thoroughly resent and reject such Christian forgiveness. Rather we want Christianity to cleanse itself! I am not speaking against Christianity but for it." [12]

The height of acerbity is another letter—this one addressed to rabbis—writen by Dr. Dagobert Runes, a loner, a Jew who does not represent even the smallest faction of American Jewry. Here are some characteristic quotes: "While the Ecumenists have gifted to us the Trojan Horse of their charitable homilies on Judaeo-Christian unity, creating in the uninformed the impres-

[11] *The Reconstructionist,* October 1965, p. 3.
[12] Quoted from a privately circulated copy of the letter, pp. 3 and 6.

sion that these Dialogues in schools and community centers would make an end to 'misunderstanding' among the two great religions, the Catholic Church refused to make the slightest change in its New Testament, which contains a veritable well of Jew hate. . . . This New Testament contains 102 basic references to the Hebrew people, every one of which is viciously anti-Semitic. . . . Such is the religion every Catholic, and of course Protestant, boy and girl absorbs while reading the New Testament. . . . [Christians] may think of their Bible as a book of love; to us Jews it is a book of hate. . . . We do not want any further lessons from the Christian churches. All we want is for them to take out from their scriptures the obvious anti-Semitic references to the people of Israel and to stop teaching their children that we are the devil's brood." [13]

In my earlier article (*Concilium*, Vol. 24, pp. 152-155), I dealt with the accusation that the New Testament is anti-Semitic and thus responsible for *all* the sufferings of Jews. Hence, I need not linger with the author's pugnacious remarks. But I think it my duty to inform the reader that Dr. Runes has not left it at that —he has published his own edition of St. John's Gospel, with every allegedly anti-Jewish verse expunged. Dr. Runes is never detained by pangs of modesty, hence he can write on the book's jacket: "Edited in conformity with the true ecumenical spirit of Pope John XXIII by Dagobert D. Runes. The message of Jesus

---

[13] From a privately circulated letter, pp. 2-3, a letter that but repeats the sentiments of the author's printed tract: "The Jews and the Cross." After having completed this report I learn that, at a recent gathering of Jewish, Protestant, and Catholic scholars in Boston, U.S.A., the distinguished editor of *Judaism*, Rabbi Steven S. Schwarzchild, remarked that the appointment of Bishop Carli to a high Vatican post proves once more the dishonesty of Catholics and of the Council's declaration. The source of this rumor is, no doubt, the letter of Dr. Runes who maintains that "Paul VI . . . appointed Bishop Luigi Carli, a renowned anti-Semitic essayist, to head the Curia into whose hands the fate of the 'Jewish problem' was entrusted". I am not astonished at this falsification of facts—it is not the only one in the letter. But I was obviously wrong in calling Dr. Runes a loner. The ready acceptance of his letter by a man of Dr. Schwarzchild's caliber shows that there are other Jews besides Dr. Runes who like to pollute the fresh air Christians and Jews now breathe.

is offered here without adulteration by hate and revulsion against the people of the Savior."

Happy Voices

Lest I give the impression that these instances of rancor typify Jewish response to the Declaration, I should like to quote two favorable reactions. The first is by Dr. Ernst Ludwig Ehrlich: "Despite several discordant notes . . . the Council's Declaration 'on the Jewish religion' made theological progress. This advance becomes quite clear when one compares the Declaration with the 'resolution on anti-Semitism' by the World Council of Churches (New Delhi, 1961). One must gladly acknowledge that the latter takes a determined stand against anti-Semitism. Yet, it contains an obvious missionary element. Jews are viewed here, not as 'separated brethren', rather the complete abolition of anti-Semitism is to create the condition for a turning of the Jews to Christ. . . .

"In a very decisive way, the Declaration points toward the future when all men will call upon the *one* Lord who first appeared to Israel, the one Lord whom at the end all men will serve shoulder to shoulder. This is Israel's hope, and the Church makes it her own. Thus, Christians and Jews have in common not only the foundations of a biblical past but also the one great destiny, the reign of the one God over all the children of men. The Declaration underlines this common hope. It shuns every allusion to Israel's conversion which would have offended the Jews and deepened the chasm between Christians and Jews. Nevertheless, the Church did not fail to give the witness demanded of her. Together with the Jews, then, she hopes that the road into the future will be happier than the experience of Christians and Jews in the past." [14]

Most Jews have little chance to make their opinions known,

[14] From a lecture, "What is the Significance of the Second Vatican Council for us Jews," part of a series called *Was bedeutet das Zweite Vatikanische Konzil für uns?* Basel, 1966, p. 209-215.

in fact, they avoid the public forum. It may therefore be informative to relate a personal experience. Earlier this year, I spoke before a traditional Jewish congregation on the common ground of Judaism and Christianity and on the view of Judaism that emerges from the Declaration. The next day, the Rabbi wrote me: "We stand deeply indebted to you for having pointed out to us something which is so obvious and which bears retelling again and again. To have brought into focus the common heritage that both Jew and Christian possess is something that must now be proclaimed from the housetops, so that it will permeate the air we breathe and seep down into the hearts and minds of our people so that peace—genuine peace—will be achieved."

Why, Why, Why?

The question remains, why have many Jews reacted to the Jewish Statement with ill temper and asperity? As I see it, there are several answers. First. In the past, Jews had, as a rule, to conceal, even repress, their bitterness over the abuse and injustice they had to bear. When the Council changed the climate of Christian-Jewish relations, the pent-up emotions did not vanish —in many instances the long held down anger simply exploded. Thus all kinds of grievances came to the fore—some justified, some not—grievances of whose existence most Christians were unaware. Sad though this appears, its long range effect may be wholesome. The release of wounded feelings, the freedom to voice their rancor may in the end prove to be a much needed catharsis. With fear and anger purged, trust and healthy self-esteem may be strengthened, and the newly found serenity may then be fruit of the Declaration.

Second. An exaggerated self-esteem may be at work that is the opposite of serene self-confidence, easily degenerating into self-worship. In an entirely different context—that of the Harvard "Colloquium on Judaism and Christianity" of October 1966 —Markus Barth noticed "on the side of the Jewish partners [to that dialogue] repeated signs of an emerging triumphalism, which raised its head in three forms: 1. Christianity was called a sinking ship, an incident within Jewish history, hardly worthy of further notice let alone conversation. . . . 2. The immense suffering and the abysmal horrors of Auschwitz were called to mind in order to prove the superiority of the witness rendered by the suffering Jews. . . . 3. An unprejudiced study of post-biblical Judaism . . . reveals that Christianity has no other and no better way of righteousness to offer than that which 'sensitive' Judaism has always upheld. . . . Not by Christians but by a Jewish speaker was this attitude labelled 'triumphalism'." [15]

Third. Another psychological mechanism explains not so much the resentment but the dissatisfaction of some Jewish spokesmen. Recently, Arthur Hertzberg, a noted American Rabbi, wrote that when the Jewish Statement appeared, the assumption was that it would be almost universally hailed. The large majority of Jews, and of their leaders, do indeed welcome the action of the bishops in Council. In order to understand why some do not, one has to remember that when, two centuries ago, Jews began to leave the ghetto legally and physically, they carried it with them as a psychological reality. They felt they were still inside an embattled bastion. So much so that a sense of rallying against the enemy seemed the ultimate factor that bound Jews—believing and non-believing Jews—together.

But now that the end of Christian anti-Semitism is in sight, Jewish self-identity seems threatened. Though American Jews, like all Jews, abhorred massive anti-Semitism, they somehow considered a little anti-Semitism a good thing because it kept them together. The new climate in Christian-Jewish relations leads to the question: "What do Jews really believe in strongly enough, in their overwhelming majority, to make them want to continue their community and their tradition?"

Rabbi Hertzberg concluded with this beautiful thought: The ways of God are strange. The travail of Jews had a deep influence on the rethinking of Catholics now going on. This rethink-

---

[15] From an editorial "Dialogue is not Enough" in *Journal of Ecumenical Studies,* Vol. 4 (Winter 1967) 116. The problem of space forces me to these meagre excerpts. I hope the readers of *Concilium* will consult the entire editorial.

ing, however, opens within the Jewish community all kinds of new questions, or reopens old ones shunted aside. "I am mystic enough to believe that each of us is an instrument in God's hands for the remaking of the other." [16]

A Seed of Hope

No small fruit of the Declaration is a moving exchange of letters that appeared in *Le Monde* of Paris. Speaking as if the long range results of the Declaration were already accomplished, Michel Elyor-Friedmann of Beersheba (Israel) rejoiced: "A great step has just been taken. . . . Catholic prayers have been cleansed of every term offensive to Jews." He went on: "Is it not high time that Jews be inspired by this example to examine themselves and see in all objectivity, in all conscience, where things stand with their own prayers?" He then cited among other passages the one from the Passover Haggadah "where one demands of God to pour out his wrath upon all those peoples who do not know him and to cut them off". The world would have been quickly depopulated if God had lent his ear to such petitions, he claimed, and wondered why it was so necessary to hurl an anathema against peoples who do not acknowledge the God of the Bible, and why his service should demand that they be cursed. Are they really so blameworthy that one must call the fury of heaven on them because they practice and live a faith that is not ours? "It would be a good thing," he mused, "if a council, this time a Jewish one, gathered . . . for the purpose of rooting out every seed of hatred toward man, whoever he may be. . . . For the virus of hate is transmitted from the tender infancy of one generation to that of another. . . . A ray of universal love, too, if started in the earliest childhood, would be a catalyst among peoples, among all the peoples." [17]

In her answer of January 13, 1966, Mme. Eliane Amado Lévy-Valensi voiced her fear that, in Mr. Elyor-Friedmann's letter, a concern for symmetry has faulted the much deeper

[16] *The National Catholic Reporter*, 4/12/67.
[17] *Le Monde*, 12/28/1966.

concern for reciprocity. She then made the following points:

"(a) One cannot compare the cry of distress uttered by the persecuted to the dogmatic condemnation of the victims by the persecutor. Israel has always carried on the symbolic struggle of David against Goliath. . . .

"(b) No doubt, one can suppress certain texts but can one suppress psalm verses, prophetic utterances—the common patrimony of the Jewish and the Christian communities—chanted and recited by one as well as the other? The verses to which M. Elyor-Friedmann refers are, among others, these: 'Pour out your wrath upon the nations that acknowledge you not' (Ps. 78 [79]:6). 'Pour out your wrath upon them; let the fury of your anger overtake them' (Ps. 68 [69]:25).

"(c) It is not enough to know these appeals, one must also look at their context, at their reason. The latter is given in Ps. 78 [79]:7: 'For they have devoured Jacob and laid waste his dwelling.' Thus it is faithlessness that is given up to destruction, it is the murdered, the one who denies God by his attack on man. One cannot understand these texts at all if one sees the Judaism that speaks through them as though it were a dogma; one cannot understand them unless one takes them as existential outpourings of real men."

After having posited a moving, though sometimes arbitrary, affinity, if not identity, between Jesus and Israel through the ages, Mme. Lévy-Valensi stated that these cries of seeming hatred were really cries of anguish and, no less, professions of faith: "When the enemy surrounds me, with the help of the Lord I will tear him to pieces." They are stubborn affirmations of hope in an unequal battle against evil and death as it is waged by every man, but in an essential and exemplary manner, by Israel and by Jesus whom Pastor Jean Lacocque calls "the central Jew".

Though one ought not suppress these texts, Mme. Lévy-Valensi continued, one must certainly wash them of all hate. One must consider them as moments of a painful struggle, landmarks and stages of a historic memory whose mission it is to beget love in the very encounter with hatred. In this spirit, she told of a startling experience: "One of my friends, returned from Auschwitz, overheard an old dying Jew. In his prayers the old Jew spontaneously discovered the saying of Jesus he had not known: 'Forgive them, Lord, they do not know what they do.' " [18]

[18] *Le Monde*, 1/19/1967.

PART II
BIBLIOGRAPHICAL
SURVEY

Petrus Huizing, S.J./*Louvain, Belgium*

Crime and Punishment in the Church

All the authors that have dealt in general with the revision of Canon Law stress the need for a thorough re-casting of the fifth section, the penal code (*De delictis et poenis*). They particularly insist that it should be radically simplified. There are, however, but a few publications that deal specifically with this revision of the penal code.[1] What follows is a critical survey of the basic problems raised in those studies. I do not propose to discuss purely technical questions, such as terminology and method.

In the whole question of the renewal of Church order the revision of this penal code is one of the hardest nuts to crack. Yet, the maintenance or rather restoration of an ecclesiastical discipline is the necessary obverse of the positive expectations

[1] See, J. Baldanza, "De recognoscendo iure canonico poenali quaestiones quaedam;" "De iure canonico poenali secundum hodiernam ecclesiologiam recognoscendo," both in *Ephemerides iuris canonici* 19 (1963), pp. 93-104 and 20 (1964), pp. 3-17; cf. 21 (1965), p. 64ff.; O. Cassola, "De jure poenali Codicis canonico emendando"; and "Natura e divisione del delitto: osservazioni de jure condendo," both in *Apollinaris* 32 (1959), pp. 240-59 and 34 (1961), pp. 332-44; R. Castillo Lara, "Algunas reflexiones sobre la futura reforma del Libro V C.I.C.," in *Salesianum* 23 (1961), pp. 317-38; A. Scheuermann, "Erwägungen zur kirchlichen Strafrechtsreform," in *Archiv für katholisches Kirchenrecht* 131 (1962), pp. 393-415; A. Szentirmai, "Quaestiones de iure poenali canonico hodiernis necessitatibus accommodando," in *Monitor Ecclesiasticus* 87 (1962), pp. 607-24.

raised by Vatican Council II with regard to the image of the People of God in the present world. The Church's witness in the contemporary world consists primarily in the real Christian life of the faithful. A proclamation of the Word that cannot rely on this witness and does not find there a guarantee of its authenticity and veracity lacks persuasion. The ecclesiastical communities cannot let the mystery of salvation be celebrated or ecclesiastical posts be occupied by people who openly reject their gospel or whose conduct denies this proclamation openly and clearly. The Churches cannot be and remain themselves if they do not maintain themselves in a true unity of faith, a true unity of community and a true unity of evangelical life. It is obviously not a matter of taking disciplinary measures against every expression of human weakness or sinfulness. But it *is* a matter of not jeopardizing the essential unity in faith, communion and Christian life of the ecclesiastical communities.

It is generally agreed that the penal law contained in the present Code of Canon Law is for a large part totally out of date, and moreover a dead letter. To apply it means in most cases a complication of the confessor's job, although it is in no way his business to look after the maintenance of the Church's discipline. It can be said without exaggeration that today there exists no clear public discipline in the Churches. To give but one example: What can a hierarchy, who in their province proclaim social justice as the most urgent of Christian obligations, do in the way of practical disciplinary measures about Catholics who, in public, quite frankly disregard this obligation in their actions? And how can such a proclamation be taken seriously if precisely such Catholics fully participate in the liturgical celebrations of the Church, or are even given a place of honor there?

In such a situation one can obviously not draft a system of penal laws sitting behind one's desk and hope that this by itself will restore or introduce discipline in all the Churches. All one can do is to set up a few basic principles about discipline in the Churches, and to indicate some directives, rather than precise rules, which may help the Churches in their effort to maintain a reasonable discipline. Here, too, a relatively long period of experimentation will be necessary before we can put together a system of norms that are genuinely workable in the Church's life.

Penal Law or Discipline?

To prove that the Church needs a penal code it has been argued that coercive power (*potestas coactiva*) is just as necessary to the Church as law at large. It is said that the Church is a perfect society (*societas perfecta*) and that this requires an external juridical ordering of the life of the community. Coercion is an essential element of law, or at least a necessary aspect of it. It is admitted that canonical punishment must be used with caution today, not for intrinsic reasons but because today's world has become so indifferent.

This point of view applies to Church order a concept of law that is valid for law and order in secular States but not for the Church. It is true that in earlier days excommunication and other punitive measures of the Church had a pronounced co-ercive character, first of all, because in the religiously homoge-neous society of those days these measures were backed by public opinion, and because if the transgressor resisted such ecclesi-astical measures he would ultimately have to face the "secular arm". But even in those days, certainly in current teaching, the emphasis fell on the essentially religious and ecclesiastical mean-ing of such measures. They wanted to bring the transgressor to conversion and penance, and to protect the religious community against attacks on their faith or the order of their communal life.

The principle of religious freedom accepted by the Council now forces us to abandon every form of social coercion, also within the Church. Membership of this community, participation in the liturgical celebrations and the Church's apostolic mission, the acceptance and execution of ecclesiastical offices and services —all this the Church can only wish to have on an exclusively voluntary basis. Any measures by which the Church excludes somebody from this community, from the right to liturgical participation or from the exercise of an ecclesiastical office, can only be meant today as measures to maintain the community of worship and proclamation, first in actual fact, then also verbally, as an authentic and credible sign in this world. The Church will obviously hope that her judgment will bring possible transgressors to a change of heart, but this, too, must be wholly voluntary and not as the result of coercive discipline. Thus, for instance, social and financial disadvantages that may go with being deposed from an ecclesiastical office can no longer be used as a means by which to force submission and conversion. We should rather try to cut out such consequences within what is reasonable.

It would appear to be more logical to drop the whole idea of "penal law" in the Church and to talk rather of a disciplinary Church order. Such an order is not so much concerned with judging or condemning the individual as with judging what kind of conduct would be incompatible with the nature and mission of the ecclesiastical community.

The Notion of "Offence" (Delictum)

According to Canon 2195 "offence" means in Canon Law an external and morally imputable transgression of a law or command to which a canonical sanction is added, or at least a threat of punishment, even though this punishment is not yet determined. One might conclude from this that the Church order works on the principle that there is no punishment without law (*nulla poena sine lege*), at least in the sense that no one can be punished unless the law or command states beforehand that a particular conduct is punishable. Canon 2222, par. 1, however, seems to qualify this with an exception. It says that, even though the law contains no sanction whatever, the legitimate authority can nevertheless punish the transgression of such a law, even without the threat of a sanction beforehand, if this were deemed necessary on account of public scandal or the particular seriousness of the transgression; otherwise the guilty person cannot be punished unless there has been a previous warning with threat of punishment in case of transgression. Hence, it has been suggested that either the canonical notion of "offence" should be widened or, on the contrary, that any possibility of inflicting punishment without previous determination of the punishment should be cut out. It has even been suggested that this determination should be contained in the law, so that an order could no longer contain a threat of punishment. Here reference is made to the legislation prevailing in many countries and to the Declaration of Human Rights that contains this principle.

Now, the principle that a judge cannot inflict punishment unless he acts on an existing penal law, fits in very well with a system where legislature and judicature are separate functions. Then it is up to the legislator to lay down what punishment must accompany what transgression, and the judge has but to apply these laws. But in Church order there is no separation in principle between legislature and judicature, and particularly not in penal law. Exclusively penal processes do not occur in ecclesiastical courts. Disciplinary measures are in fact taken by the various bodies of Church government. Theoretically and practically it is a moot point whether this *can* be changed, and whether such a change is desirable.

It is also a moot point whether, particularly in an ecclesiastical community, it is desirable to include a complete list of all offences with their respective sanctions in a legal code which is valid for the whole Church or for the whole Latin and Eastern Churches respectively. In civilian society such certainty about the law must exist in order that citizens may know exactly what kind of conduct may lead to a penal court case. But has this certainty any meaning in an ecclesiastical community? Is a Catholic entitled to recognition as a full member of the community in spite of serious misconduct simply because such conduct has not been foreseen by the law? But there is sense in laying down that no member of the Church can be exposed to disciplinary measures without previous warning. It also makes sense to establish a procedure for the taking of such measures, which will protect members against every injustice and arbitrariness. The Church can hardly offer her members certainty about the law in the sense of impunity in all cases unless they are precisely determined in the law. But she can give them reasonable certainty that they will not suffer injustice and arbitrary behavior. And then we can conveniently forget about a legal definition of "offence".

Discipline and Penance

In commentaries on this same Canon 2195, par. 1, and the definition of an ecclesiastical "offence" it is said, on the one hand, that in penal law the Church only considers the social aspects of the offence, not the aspect of "sin" for which one is responsible to God and which the Church deals with in the sacrament of penance with so-called "vicarious authority" (*potestas vicaria*). Here satisfaction is obtained through a voluntarily accepted penance. In the same way, when other people's rights have been injured, it is dealt with, not in a criminal court but in a civil court; it is only subject to sanctions as a matter of public order. On the other hand, when these authors explain the words "external offence" (*violatio externa*) in this canon, they say that "external" is not the same as "public". Thus, for instance, apostasy, which is "external" in one way or another but not publicized, is punished by excommunication. Some canonists then still try to maintain that a secret apostasy still affects public order somehow but obviously without convincing anybody.

We start here, on the one hand, from the right principle that penal law or the disciplinary order of the Church is by nature a public matter, a matter that concerns the community. On the other hand, we have here disciplinary measures about conduct that is not public, and this cannot be reconciled with the principle. Here we have therefore an indication that the development of a principle has not yet been completed. There is indeed the principle that the Church's concern for the life of the community should be separated from her concern for individual members, and this principle is only gradually coming to be realized in Church order. For instance, the secret of confession has only gradually become as absolute as it is today. Ecclesiastical administration is becoming increasingly distinct in principle from functions that are concerned with personal spiritual direction.

Strong pleas have been made that this distinction should also be consistently applied to ecclesiastical penal law. It seems to me that Scheuermann is right when he says that the restoration of penal law as dealing with public order is the most fundamental requirement for a revision of this penal code. But then, it seems to me, we must begin with cutting out the whole notion of a "secret offence".

The Notion of "Punishment"

A consistent application of the distinction between discipline and penance should also bring about a modification of the notion of canonical punishment. Canon 2215 describes ecclesiastical punishment as the deprivation of a good to bring about the correction of the delinquent and satisfaction for the offence. In the secular State all penal measures are measures with which the community, through its competent bodies, threatens the transgressor. There is not a single system where the transgressor must himself apply punishment to himself. It is different in Canon Law. Here excommunication, suspension and interdict are not only measures that the community or the ecclesiastical authority takes against the transgressor, but also an obligation on the transgressor to execute these measures himself. Ecclesiastical punishment not only obliges the Churches not to let somebody approach the sacraments, or to administer them, or to let him partake in the celebration of the eucharist, or to exercise a function, etc., but also imposes upon the transgressor himself the duty to abstain from these actions in conscience. We should seriously consider whether we should not turn all ecclesiastical disciplinary measures into sanctions that only the Church or the Churches execute, and should not superimpose positive obligations on the delinquent. What he thinks he can or cannot do in his private life and by the light of his own conscience, is a matter between him and God or between him and the Church in the sacrament of penance exclusively, where some judgment shall have to be reached. It seems no longer necessary nor desirable that some-body should, apart from his obligation in conscience to abstain from the sacraments or specific priestly functions, should be burdened with obligations of positive law on top of that. This, of course, does not affect the duty in conscience to submit him-self to the just measures taken by the competent authority, in the same way as he must submit himself to the just punishment of the civil authority.

In this way we can also avoid a contradiction on this point in the existing discipline and Canon Law. When the Church de-cides that somebody must be denied communion or the celebra-tion of Mass for public misconduct, she does not judge the man's conscience and does not intend to judge this. "The Church does not judge of matters of conscience" (*de internis Ecclesia non iudicat*) is a centuries-old adage. But in that case it is bad logic to impose a *direct* obligation of conscience on somebody to take disciplinary measures against himself, and not only *indirectly* the duty in conscience to submit himself to a just judgment and not to resist just measures taken by the authority. Whether some-body in his private life and in conscience is worthy to receive communion or celebrate Mass, he should judge himself and in confession his confessor; whether one can administer communion to somebody or allow him to celebrate Mass, is the Church's judgment. Obviously, one has to take account of the Church's judgment when judging a question of conscience, but the pub-lic judgment of the Church should not be at the same time a judgment in conscience.

If one can agree with this point of view, the disciplinary measures of the Church, like the penal measures taken by the State, will directly determine the conduct of the community toward the delinquent, but only indirectly the conduct of the delinquent himself. In that case the function of Canon Law is to regulate the public aspect of the life of the community, not the private life of a person. This would be the logical application of the separation of law from conscience (*forum externum* from *forum internum*).

Retribution and Correction

Canon 2216 distinguishes between correction (*poenae medicinales*) or censures, which are more directly aimed at the reform of the delinquent, and retribution (*poenae vindicativae*), which is aimed at punishment for an offence. It has been argued that these two kinds of measures are not essentially different in aim. The only difference would be that corrective measures cease through absolution as soon as the delinquent admits that he has done wrong, while the retributive measures do the same either through the running out of the term set by the sanctions or, before that, through dispensation.

Until the 15th century neither Church law nor the science of Canon Law knew of this distinction. From various texts the classical authors built up a more or less adequate notion of censures. Not until the Code of 1917 was an effort made to make a clear distinction. If we want to see in Church order not so much a penal law aimed at the person of the delinquent as a discipline aimed at the protection of the community, there would be no reason any more for a distinction between measures aimed at correction and measures aimed at retribution. All disciplinary measures aim first and foremost directly at the maintenance of the nature and unity of the Churches, and only indirectly at correction or penalization. Such measures will cease to be operative as soon as the first aim no longer requires them.

Punishment Inflicted by Law

According to Canon 2217, par. 1, 2°, a punishment imposed by law (*poena latae sententiae*) is a particular punishment so attached to a law or command that it is incurred *ipso facto* by the trangression of the law or command. It is opposed to a punishment which must result from the pronouncement of a sentence (*poena ferendae sententiae*) in which case the punishment laid down in law or command is only incurred by the sentence of a judge or a pronouncement by the authority. Most canonical punishments today are *latae sententiae*. In the Code there are at least 49 excommunications *latae sententiae* over against 5 *ferendae sententiae;* there are moreover 9 suspensions and 3 interdicts *latae sententiae.* Various arguments have been adduced to justify the existence of such punishments. In his Bull, *Auctorem Fidei,* August 28, 1794, Pius IX condemned the proposition: ". . . by natural law and divine law an excommunication and a suspension must necessarily be preceded by a personal investigation; hence, measures which contain a punishment incurred by the very fact of transgression have no more validity than that of a serious threat with punishment, without immediate effect." And one points to the constant practice during many centuries where the Church applied this kind of punishment. They are said to be a perfect means to punish at once certain offences which, because of their seriousness and the scandal caused, demand such an immediate punishment. They would even be more useful to punish offences committed in secret, and which the judge cannot punish (Canon 1933, par. 1), and which are usually not punished by authority; for instance, the offence of a confessor who absolves his accomplice in sexual sins. The Church would not primarily consider the offence as the violation of the rights of other people; moreover, it is not only public offences that should be punished. In a spiritual community punishments *latae sententiae* might be meaningful because, over and above the keeping of the law, the members are expected to live by the inner conviction of their faith. Such punishments would even be necessary because otherwise a pronouncement by authority or judge would be required for all individual cases of apostasy, bigamy, education of children outside the Church, etc.

Many objections, however, are also brought in against punishments *latae sententiae.* These take no account of various degrees of responsibility. The legislator does not know the transgressor, the judge does, can make personal contact with him and adjust the punishment to his condition. The transgressor must also decide for himself in his own conscience whether he has incurred the penalty or not, and this judgment is often difficult, even for the confessor. That hidden offences remain unpunished is of no great importance. Punishments are not primarily aiming at individuals but at the public order of the community. They must correspond to the social consequences of the offences. They are not imposed in order to burden the conscience of the transgressor but in order to protect the community. It is precisely these sanctions *latae sententiae* which caused penal law to shift from public order to private penance and the conscience. If somebody has incurred such a penalty in secret, he is not obliged to follow it up if this jeopardizes his good name (Canons 2261 and 2284). The confessor can always absolve, not only from the secretly incurred penalty, but even from public censure (Canon 2251). And thus the penalty has become a private affair; no longer a matter for the community but a personal matter, a tail-end to sin. Sanctions are dealt with by the confessors. Because of all these objections there is a general desire that punishments *latae sententiae* should be drastically reduced. No author as yet has proposed total abolition in writing, but there are some canonists who would support this.

The idea of a punishment *latae sententiae* was only developed in the Middle Ages by Scholastic canonists. Earlier texts, sometimes adduced in support, do not yet know of this. When the Council of Antioch of 341 declared that those who dared to take the meaning out of a decree of the Council of Nicaea would be excommunicated and cast out of the Church if they were laymen, and would be outside the Church if clerical; or when the Council of Orange of 538 laid down that a cleric, guilty of some specific offences must abstain from communion for a definite time, or not exercise his function, one should remember that in those days there was still a public penance which did not yet make a clear distinction between a public discipline and a non-public sacramental penance. Such decisions could, in those days, mean at the same time disciplinary measures of the Church if the offence was public, and obligations which *ipso facto* affected the transgressor's conscience if the offence was hidden.

The question is whether a secretly incurred penalty which adds obligations of positive law to the duties of conscience incurred *ipso facto* by the violation of Church order, has still got any meaning today. The faithful, layman or priest, who is conscious of a grave offence, knows that he must confess this to the Church; that without conversion and readiness to confess he should not receive the sacraments; that, as the old saying goes, he is excommunicated before God, and that he has put himself outside the living community of the faithful in Christ. He knows that the Church judges the matter in this way and that he is subject to that judgment. Why then burden his conscience by adding canonical sanctions? And why burden the confessors with having to absolve from disciplinary measures?

Some authors want to maintain the punishments *latae sententiae* at least for specific misconduct in office by priests, where this conduct is by its very nature not public, as in the case of giving sacramental absolution to an accomplice in sins against the commandment of chastity, or of a direct violation of the confessional secret. Such offences can create grave scandal and seriously injure the religious life of others. This, of course, is true. But is there any practical point in reacting against this by excommunications that are just as secret as the offences? One might consider a limitation of the power to absolve to particular experts who can help such confrères effectively instead of giving this power to all confessors. There would also be a point in denying priests the power to absolve their accomplices (and why is this limited to sexual offences?) and in seeing to it that the faithful know that this power is thus limited. But as long as violations of the priestly office are not public, it is difficult to see why the situation should become still more complicated by secret disciplinary measures.

The Prohibition to Absolve

One of the effects of excommunication is that sacramental absolution must neither be given nor received. It seems to me that this is still a hang-over from that lack of distinction between public discipline and private penance. Castillo Lara has suggested dropping this prohibition as an ecclesiastical sanction. If all disciplinary measures are taken by the public ecclesiastical authority and removed by the same authority, instead of by the confessor, such a prohibition would no longer be justified. For this would mean that the delinquent cannot receive the sacrament of penance before the authority has withdrawn the prohibition while in fact he is entitled to sacramental absolution as soon as he is in the right disposition.

To this one might add that the Church's judgment of the necessity of disciplinary measures against a member, cannot be, and does not intend to be, a judgment of his conscience. He should therefore be free to deal personally with matters of conscience, even in confession, independently of his public and canonical position in the community.

Excommunication

The Code (Canon 2257, par. 1) describes excommunication as a censure or corrective punishment by which someone is excluded from the community of the faithful. The following canons list the effects of this sanction: loss of the right to come to the Church's services, except for preaching; no active participation in Church services; no reception of sacraments; no reception of sacramentalia; no ecclesiastical burial; loss of indulgences and public intercession of the Church; no share in so-called legal ecclesiastical actions such as the management of Church property, functioning in the Church's judicature, being a godparent at baptism or confirmation, voting in ecclesiastical elections; no reception or execution of sacred orders; no administrative functions, etc. Not every excommunication entails the whole list, and some only become operative after sentence.

Anyone who reads this list for the first time will wonder how one penalty can possibly have so many and such varied results all at once. This all-embracing excommunication is not an institution which has existed in the Church since the beginning. Formerly, when excommunication had become something definite, it was divided into several kinds, each with its own definite and limited effects. Total excommunication is probably connected with those old all-embracing penalties like civil death, outlawry and exile. Should the Church maintain penalties that embrace excommunication and other measures *en bloc*? Should we not try to introduce a different principle today, a principle that might be formulated as follows: When it seems necessary that several disciplinary measures must be taken at the same time against a member, the necessity for each measure should be considered separately, and the reasons for each should be stated in the sentence.

It is also doubtful whether all these effects still make sense today. Anyone can visit a Catholic Church and come to the services, which are, moreover, all a kind of "preaching", without needing any "right" to it; why then should this be denied to a Catholic? Active participation in Church services will also have to be seen in another light than formerly since all the faithful are supposed to take an active part nowadays. It has already been suggested that the prohibition to give absolution should be abolished. The same might well apply to the prohibition of communion in danger of death and for the sacrament of the sick. Elsewhere I have argued that no ecclesiastical measure should forbid or obstruct the validity of a marriage. The loss of a share in indulgences and intercession appears to have lost most of its meaning. Whether the Church's prayers will be able to help someone depends on his disposition. Here again, a disciplinary measure is strengthened with a consequence that belongs rather to the conscience and disposition of the individual person.

Public Administration of Justice

Of the 17 recommendations unanimously accepted by the Canon Law Society of America in October, 1965 the 9th runs as follows: "That the penal laws be drastically curtailed and simplified and that their application, for the greater part, be placed in the hands of the local ordinary or regional and national conferences of bishops." And the 10th: "That an accused person be not punished unless he is aware of the nature of the accusation, the identity of his accuser, and the evidence of the truth of the accusation, and he has adequate opportunity to defend himself." These recommendations wholly correspond to the view that the discipline of the Church is a public discipline, and that ecclesiastical disciplinary measures are a reaction against anti-ecclesiastical conduct, the expression of the will of the community to maintain itself and its own character. If this meaning must be socially evident these measures must be taken by and in that ecclesiastical community which is immediately affected in the matter. Local authorities are therefore indicated, not the distant authorities at the center.

This means, first of all, the diocesan bishop or someone who represents him in such matters (a vicar for affairs of discipline). A public procedure in the sense that everyone knows about it will not be desirable in many cases, but it *is* desirable in the sense that those who do the judging genuinely represent the community and that their judgment should reflect the judgment of the community not only in a formally juridical way but also in terms of social reality. Some very classical and ancient institutions could serve as example. One can find a juridical procedure with the cooperation of the whole community, for instance, in such early collections of canons as the *Apostolic Constitutions*. The denial of participation in the eucharist as pronounced, for instance, by the pastoral council of a deanery or a diocese, would be felt far more deeply as conveying the witness of the community than if only the bishop or the episcopal court pronounced this sentence. It would also be necessary to guarantee the appeal to a higher court, e.g., the episcopal conference or a national or regional pastoral council, or a council of priests where priests are concerned. The first centuries already knew of such appeals from the verdict of a bishop to a provincial synod.

Most of what has been said here in order to stimulate discussion among the experts, has been for a large part negative. My suggestions have dealt with those things that ought not to appear

in Church discipline rather than with those that ought to be
written in. But positive, really workable norms for discipline
will come rather from practice and experiment. This practice and
these experiments must no doubt be guided by general principles,
and it is worth trying to establish such principles. But general
principles alone do not by themselves provide an authentic disciplinary order for a living community.

Ivan Žužek, S.J./*Rome, Italy*

Opinions on the Future Structure of Oriental Canon Law

How should one frame the future Oriental Code so that there will be unity in essentials and diversity in accidentals? How should one embody certain momentous and essential principles that have arisen out of the promulgation of the *Decree on Oriental Catholic Churches;* such as the greater autonomy of Oriental Churches, the rights of patriarchs, the obligation to preserve ancient traditions, and the necessity for modern adaptation? How does one propose and enunciate such delicate points as the role of the "Uniate Churches", the possibility of recognizing the jurisdiction of the Orthodox hierarchy, and the need for different Churches in the same locality to harmonize their disciplinary practices? These and other major issues are now being seriously discussed in recent literature on Oriental Canon Law. The present article attempts to examine the main opinions, which open new perspectives for a future Oriental codification, with the hope that this may assist the growing ecumenical movement for Christian unity.[1]

[1] The page references in brackets refer to the works listed in the bibliography at the end of the article. The bibliography is divided under the same headings as the article itself.

A. THE COMMISSION FOR THE ORIENTAL CODE

The Pontifical Commission for the Revision of the *Codex iuris canonici* is composed of 60 members, all cardinals, two secretaries and 70 advisers. The Commission for the Oriental Code has at present 12 members, one assistant, and four advisers. Among the members are six Oriental patriarchs (Sidarous, Tappouni, Maximos IV, Meouchi, Cheikho, Batanian), the Ukrainian Major Archbishop Slipyj, and five curial cardinals (Cicognani, Agagianian, Tisserant, Larraona, Heard). It may be noted that the chairman of the Commission, Cardinal Agagianian, was also an Oriental patriarch until his abdication, August 27, 1962, and that Cardinals Tisserant and Cicognani were for many years secretaries of the Sacred Congregation for Oriental Churches. When this Commission was instituted in 1935, it had five members, a secretary, and twelve advisers. In 1962 the advisers were only seven, of whom three (Dib, Herman, Goyeneche) have since died. The official task of the Commission was, and still is, to compile a Code for the Oriental Churches; today, however, it must also undertake the revision of the parts of this Code already edited. The work accomplished by the Commission was thorough and extensive, resulting in the promulgation (1949-1957) of four *Motu proprios* containing 1590 canons: the laws on marriage, procedure, religious, temporal goods, rites, and persons. In 1958, additional canons were ready for publication and promulgation on general principles and sacraments, but they never appeared, as the approach of the Council quite naturally halted the work of compilation.

The Council brought with it an astonishing number of new pastoral, ecumenical, and ecclesiological insights touching almost every single canon both in the *Codex iuris canonici* and in the Oriental Code, not only in the promulgated sections but also in those planned.

The Commission for the Oriental Code has up to now published 58 most welcome and important volumes of sources of Oriental law. Moreover it has issued various authentic interpretations of the Code, some of which appeared in *Acta Apostolicae Sedis* (of 1953), whereas others have never been published. However, the real work of the compilation has not yet been resumed. All the reasons for this may not be apparent, but one suspects that serious work in this field will be impossible until basic principles, laid down by the Council, have been fully assimilated and established as the foundation stones for future codification. As some of these principles concern the whole Church, it is to be hoped that they will be soon elaborated by the Commission for the Revision of the *Codex iuris canonici* as their work is proceeding with all desired despatch. Four Oriental patriarchs, the Ukrainian Major Archbishop (all appointed on November 13, 1965), and a few advisers, experts on Oriental matters, represent the Oriental Churches in this Commission for a just solution of questions of universal interest. It is clear then that in this field, waiting is a necessary policy. However, it is to be hoped that this waiting does not mean that the Latin Code will once again be taken as the basis for the Oriental codification.

There are other basic questions, confined to the Christian East, the solution of which is absolutely essential for the work of codification and which may, therefore, necessitate a special commission. As far as is known nothing has been done toward a solution of these questions (discussed on the following pages), a thing that is less understandable and very vexing to canonists. The feeling that the new wine contained in conciliar documents does not fit the Oriental *ius vigens,* causes deep distress in some circles, great relief in others, but in everyone a serene hope that the shape of the future Oriental codification will in actual fact correspond to genuine Oriental traditions.

B. A Provisional and Ecumenical Codification for the "Uniate Churches"

On October 20, 1964, 7 of the Orthodox observers at the Ecumenical Council presented a *Memorandum* addressed to the pope, in which they denounced the *Schema of the Decree on the*

Oriental Churches (the word *"Catholic"* was added afterward) as being proselytizing and anti-ecumenical in character and as offensive to Orthodoxy.[2] A few points mentioned in the *Memorandum* were voiced in the interventions on the Council floor and were later proposed as amendments to the text in *modi* sent to the respective Commission. Though it is difficult to establish whether there was any interdependence between the *modi* and the *Memorandum,* it is certain that such *modi* succeeded in changing important parts of the text (the title of the *Decree,* Arts. 24 and 29) in the sense desired by the Orthodox. Nevertheless, the fundamentally negative attitude of the *Memorandum* remains the quasi-official position of Orthodoxy after the Council. However, what Murray (p. 18) says of ecumenism in general holds true, too, in this matter, that "though it is fairly easy to offer a summary of a half dozen Greek and emigré Russian theologians, it is very difficult to estimate Orthodox attitudes on a wider scale". At any rate the opposition to the Schema, which in the opinion of Dumond was "regrettable" (p. 74), was very strong at the Third Pan-Orthodox Conference at Rhodes in November, 1964. For not a few Orthodox the very existence of the "Uniate Churches" should be abolished before any serious ecumenical dialogue. Obviously, such opposition, indeed hatred in some circles, to "Uniates" makes it impossible to say or do anything in their favor which would not seem anti-ecumenical. Yet, the Council's wish, expressed in the *Decree* (Art. 1) for a renewed flourishing of the Oriental Catholic Churches, would seem to exclude the possibility of a dialogue over existence of these Churches, even though some Catholics, as, e.g., Aucagne (p. 710), would be ready to admit such dialogue. This existence is a fundamental human right, which is no smaller or greater in any Church, whether it results from such historical facts as the Council of Chalcedon (451), the Schism of 1054, the Reformation, or from reunion with the Catholic Church. The flourishing, then, of the Oriental Catholic Churches is demanded by their

[2] In the following pages *the Decree on the Catholic Oriental Churches* is quoted as *Decree.*

apostolic duty of saving souls. It means, in the first place, a profound sacramental life among their faithful and is, therefore, a thing to be desired and prayed for as the highest gift of the Holy Spirit. Indeed such a flourishing of the Churches, be they Catholic or Orthodox, is the chief preliminary postulate for Christian union, whereas a discussion on the right to existence of any Church is sterile and can lead only to greater disunion.

Dr. Vischer (p. 104) and Msgr. Chrysostomos (Constantinople) do not challenge this existence, but they express a desire for a better definition of the role of the "Uniate Churches" than that which the *Decree* seems to suppose. An interesting dialogue on this role between Msgr. Chrysostomos and Msgr. Zoghby, opposed in some points by the Maronite review *Antiochena,* was published in 1966 in *Informations Catholiques Internationales* 1966, no. 267, 28-30; 278, 26-27. Dr. Vischer would also like a clear declaration that the way to union with Orthodoxy is not necessarily through these Churches. In this connection it seems worth noting that Art. 24 of the *Decree* insists on the implementation of the *Decree on Ecumenism* and on the work for union in these Churches by means of prayer, good example, fidelity to Oriental traditions, better knowledge of the Orthodox, collaboration with them, and a fraternal attitude toward them and their opinions. This article gives no encouragement to the "proselytism", so execrated in Athens. Significant, too, is the final article of the *Decree,* which states that the legal prescriptions contained in it are provisional in character, until the full communion with the Orthodox Churches shall have been reestablished. This amounts to a declaration that the acceptance of such provisions is by no means a preliminary condition for a future union. Moreover, it seems also to imply that the Catholic Oriental Churches will have to conform, at the time of union, to the Canon Law of the Orthodox rather than the opposite. Abbot Hoeck, in his commentary on the *Decree* (p. 391), best expressed the malaise that the *Decree* has created in the ecumenical field, saying, that the ultimate solution of the problems involved will be possible only, paradoxical though it may sound, when the Churches and the hierarchies for which the *Decree* was enacted shall no longer exist, but only the Oriental and Latin Churches fraternally united, in other words, when the *Decree* itself will be unnecessary.

In what regards the future codification for the Oriental Catholic Churches, the following requirements seem to flow from the short considerations given above: (1) the codification should be based on a clear understanding of the ecumenical role of the "Uniate Churches", which should be defined through a serene dialogue with the Orthodox; (2) it should have the same provisional character as the *Decree* itself; and, (3) it should be, as far as possible, similar to the Canon Law of the non-Catholic Oriental Churches with which it will be assimilated at the time of union.

C. The Non-Binding Character of the Code for the Orthodox and the Recognition of Their Jurisdiction

It is a universally accepted teaching and one that is followed in the practice of ecclesiastical tribunals, that the Latin Code binds also non-Catholic baptized Christians, except in the case of a very few laws in which the opposite is formally stated. Huizing (p. 86), dealing with marriage law, recently advocated a radical revision in this regard as "absolutely necessary", since a positive ecclesiastical legislation for persons who do not recognize it or even know of its existence is clearly an anachronism.[3] Some canonists may still think that such an opinion is not likely to have an impact on the future Code, yet, here the *lux ex oriente* may be illuminating, which has already shone in the title of the *Decree*. Even allowing for the difference between the Orthodox and Protestants, this *lux* should nonetheless be part of the foundation of both Oriental and Latin Codes. I have (*Animadver-*

---

[3] The sixth proposal of Canon Law Society of America, of October 1965, runs as follows: "That persons who were not baptized in the Catholic Church, or who were not converted to the Catholic faith, be exempt from purely ecclesiastical laws" (*The Jurist* 26 (1965) 165).

siones, pp. 268ff.) underlined the great importance in this regard of the word "Catholic" in the title of the *Decree on Oriental Catholic Churches.* The word was added to the title at the last moment, at the request of some hundred fathers of the Council, with the express intention of excluding Orthodox from the disciplinary prescriptions of the *Decree.* In my opinion this is not just another exception from the general rule that Catholic laws bind all baptized Christians, but the abrogation of the rule itself insofar as the Orthodox are concerned. The *Decree* is in fact almost totally disciplinary, repeals many laws included in the Oriental Code, and lays down principles for its revision; it should, therefore, be considered as an integral part of the Oriental Code. Consequently, from the promulgation of the *Decree* on, the parts of the Oriental Code already issued no longer have binding force for the Orthodox, if they ever had, as was the opinion of authors like Coussa, Herman, and Faltin, who upheld the traditional view equating the Orthodox with Protestants. However, Pujol opposes this view, demonstrating by forceful arguments that even before the Council the four parts of the Oriental Code and all previous legislation for Orientals from Pius XI on were intended by the Holy See to bind exclusively Catholics. *The Jurist* 25 (1965) 306, points to the significant fact that the Holy Office gave no answer, when it was explicitly asked for a clarification of the point in 1963. Pujol has many arguments, but his main ones are based on the meaning of the term *christifideles,* to whom the four parts of the Oriental Code are addressed, and on the difference between the Orthodox and the Protestants. According to Pujol, the word *christifideles* in the documents of Pius XII signifies exclusively Catholics. As for the difference between the Orthodox and the Protestants, it is obvious to anyone reading the decrees of the Council. The Protestant communities lack a hierarchy in the strict sense of the word and are, consequently, deprived of a really binding law of their own, whereas (p. 99) the Orthodox have a rich disciplinary heritage derived from the Fathers, the Councils, and the Holy See. This heritage has never been abrogated and it is usually observed in practice by Orthodox bishops. Thus Pujol very correctly admits the binding force of the ancient canons for the Orthodox. But what should be said about those laws (and usages) issued by an Orthodox hierarchy after their separation from Rome? Many distinctions are necessary for an adequate answer to this question, but any answer depends upon the opinion one has of the validity of the jurisdiction of such a hierarchy.

Here a very important article by Bertrams is relevant. The Council has allowed freedom of discussion on this point by the concluding words of the famous *Nota praevia* that was attached to the *Constitution on the Church;* therefore, the "progressive" views have as much right to be exposed as the traditional doctrines, provided they correspond to the documents of Vatican Council II. De Vries, in his book on the Oriental Patriarchates (pp. 328-370) and in an article published in *Unitas,* 1963, with skill and great erudition, has shown how, throughout the centuries, the view has been rather that the separated bishops have no jurisdiction, though in the documents of the Holy See there is at times some hesitation about this. Bertrams, however, through an examination of the conciliar decrees, has arrived at some conclusions, which seem to merit high consideration. A few points in particular may be mentioned here. First, the communion of non-Catholic communities with the Catholic Church admits of various degrees: it is not something totally existing or totally non-existing. Secondly, episcopal consecration always confers, not only the *munus ordinis,* but also the *munus docendi* and *regendi,* which, however, cannot be exercised out of communion with the Head of the College of Bishops and its members (*Const. on the Church,* n. 21). Thirdly, the Council recognizes a *communionem hierarchicam* (p. 302) with the Orthodox Churches insofar as there exist in them elements common with the Catholic Church, not only in regard to liturgical offices and the administration of the sacraments, but also to the *munus regendi* and *docendi* (pp. 303-304). Fourthly, the Orthodox ecclesial communities are recognized as Churches, deriving from

Christ, which admit a communion with the Catholic Church, though not its fullness (p. 303). How can a real Church, even though not *pleno sensu,* exist without jurisdiction? May it be permitted to add to these conclusions of Bertrams the following questions? When one considers that the elements common to the Catholic and Orthodox Churches cover a very great range of acts, belonging to the bishop's threefold power, is it too much to assert that for all these acts Orthodox bishops enjoy a real ecclesiastical jurisdiction? If this is so, why could the new Oriental Code not recognize the binding force of laws issued by a hierarchy after its separation for all members of the respective Church? This would mean that only those acts and enactments of Orthodox hierarchs would be invalid which are contrary to scripture, Catholic teaching, or natural law. In such cases evidently there could be no "hierarchical communion" and, therefore, no valid acts.

Whatever the answer one may give to these questions and whatever one may think about the inconsistency of Bertrams' theories, one can nevertheless plead for the recognition of the jurisdiction of Orthodox hierarchies in all matters where a divergence from Catholic teaching is not involved. In an ecumenical age such a recognition does not seem to be inadmissible, as if it violated the pope's primatial power, even though it goes beyond traditional canonical concepts. It may be noted in this connection that some of the present pope's actions could be interpreted in the sense of a tacit recognition of such jurisdiction, for example, the pope's Easter Greetings published (in Russian only) in the *Moscow Patriarchal Review,* where the patriarch is greeted together "with the clergy and people entrusted to your pastoral care" and the wish is expressed to restore fraternal relations "with that portion of Christ's flock of which you are the shepherd".[4]

[4] *Žurnal Moskovskoj Patriarchii,* 1965, no. 5, 4: "k duchovenstvu i pastve, poručennym Vašemu pastyrskomu popečeniju" 1964, no. 6, 1: "s toj čast'ju stada Christova, kotoroj Vy-Pastyr".

D. Patriarchal Rights and the "Autonomy" of Churches in Oriental Canon Law

Article 9 of the *Decree* orders the restoration of the rights which Oriental patriarchs possessed at the time of union between East and West, that is for the Byzantine Church the rights of the first thousand years (until 1054). For a long time Rome and the Orientals differed on the meaning of the clause on the patriarchal rights that the Council of Florence (1439) appended to the Decree of Union: *salvis videlicet privilegiis omnibus et iuribus eorum*. For Rome the "privileges and rights" meant, more or less, the faculties granted by the Holy See contrary to common law (*C.I.C.* Can. 4); whereas for Orientals they meant that relative autonomy they thought their Churches had enjoyed for the first thousand years. It is not surprising, therefore, that this fundamental diversity of outlook prompted Rome to curtail ("auf Schritt und Tritt", says Hoeck, p. 376) patriarchal rights. As a result, Oriental Catholics were at times tempted to accuse Rome of "insincerity" for "breaking the Florentine promises", and the Orthodox have seen therein a clear justification of their mistrust of Rome. Now, however, Article 9 of the *Decree* fulfills the desires of the Orientals by stipulating that the rights of the patriarchs should correspond to "those which existed at the time of union between East and West" and that "the patriarchs with their synods constitute the highest authority for all affairs of the patriarchate, including the right of establishing new dioceses and appointing bishops . . . save for the inalienable right of the Roman pontiff to intervene in individual cases" (*in singulis casibus*).

The import of this text casts doubts on the validity of certain canons in the present Oriental Code. Some canonists, such as Pospishil (p. 34), see in Art. 9 of the *Decree* new fundamental principles that will be applicable only in a future codification concerning the rights of patriarchs and synods. Wojnar asserts (p. 203) that only those canons were abrogated which require that Rome must confirm the appointment of bishops. In my opinion (*op. cit.*, p. 280) all the canons directly contrary to Art. 9 of the *Decree* are abrogated and, probably those, too, which are contrary to its "spirit".[5] Abbot Hoeck (p. 367) claims the abrogation of the following clauses (as well as those similar to them) in regard to the rights of patriarchs and their synods: "*salva tamen Sedis Apostolicae confirmatione*", "*praevia Sedis Apostolicae approbatione*", "*obtenta Sedis Apostolicae licentia*", "*de consensu Sedis Apostolicae*", etc.

The restitution to the patriarchs of their former rights presupposes deep insight into the constitution of the Church during the first millennium. De Vries' excellent work, quoted above, indicates (pp. 19, 268-9) the scope of ecclesiastical autonomy that the patriarchs and their synods enjoyed in this period: they elected patriarchs and bishops, erected and suppressed dioceses, and regulated the whole discipline of their Churches. Rome hardly ever intervened in these matters.

To foster further research in this field, the Pontifical Oriental Institute in Rome has announced that it will conduct, from December 27-30, 1967, a congress on the subject: "The Oriental Patriarchs During the First Thousand Years." Thirteen experts, Orthodox and Catholic, have agreed to give talks on the following themes:

1. The Factors Determining the Origin of the Patriarchates (De Vries—Rome);
2. The Patriarchates and Their Autonomy (Msgr. Nabaa—Lebanon);
3. The Rights of Patriarchs, Synods, and Bishops (De Clercq—Rome);
4. The Relations Between Oriental Patriarchates (Archim. Cotsonis—Athens);
5. The Relations Between the Patriarch of Constantinople and Rome (Karagiannopoulos—Thessalonica);

[5] This article was finished on Feb. 24, 1967 and therefore could not mention the *Motu Proprio* of May 2, 1967 (cf. *Osservatore Romano*, 2-3 maggio 1967) where it is said that all canons not manifestly (*aperte*) abrogated or changed by the Council remain in force.

6. The Patriarch of Constantinople and the Emperor (Zaky-thinos—Athens);
7. The Liturgical Honors of the Byzantine Patriarch (Raes —Rome);
8. The Rights of the Bishop of Alexandria in Patristic Texts Before the Council of Chalcedon (Ortiz De Urbina—Rome);
9. The Patriarch of Antioch (Laham—Lebanon);
10. The Coptic Patriarch After the Council of Chalcedon (Masson—Cairo);
11. The Persian Catholicosate (Macomber—Baghdad);
12. The Armenian Catholicosate (Msgr. Amadouni—Paris);
13. The Bulgarian Patriarchate in the 10th Century (Dujčev —Sofia).

The importance of determining the rights of Patriarchs is highlighted by a recent event. In 1965 the Melchites elected four new bishops without approbation from Rome. Out of respect, they did not publish the names until they had informed the Holy Father. This action, although perfectly in accord with Art. 9 of the *Decree,* caused astonishment in certain circles and provoked an exchange of official letters between Rome and the Melchite patriarch. Some of these are found in the recently published *L'Église Grecque Melkite au Concile* (pp. 221ff.). They are interesting, because they indicate a present-day application and interpretation of Art. 9 of the *Decree* which will undoubtedly influence the future Oriental codification.

"Never," say the Melchites, "during the millennium through which the union of the East with the West lasted, did Rome intervene to confirm the election of an Oriental bishop," and "never will Orthodoxy accept union with Rome if it is convinced that their bishops will be named or confirmed by the Pope." [6] However, "to adapt somewhat" the ancient practice to "present-

[6] *Op. cit.,* 222: "Jamais, au cours du millénaire qu'a duré l'union de l'Orient avec l'Occident l'Évêque de Rome n'est intervenu pour confirmer l'élection d'un évêque d'Orient"; 225: "Jamais l'Orthodoxie n'acceptera l'Union si elle sait que ses évêques seront nommés ou confirmés par Rome, à l'instar des évêques latins".

day conditions" (*Decree,* Art. 9), the Melchites declare themselves ready to consult the Holy Father concerning the choice of possible candidates for the episcopate. The reason for such consultation is evident. Actually, it would be incongruous to consult "parish priests and other priests" (*Cleri sanctitati,* Can. 252) in this matter and omit consulting the Holy Father. Yet the Melchites would not like (p. 230) a juridical prescription inserted in the future Code that would impose such consultation as obligatory; for this would be contrary to the practice of the first thousand years.

The primatial right of the pope to intervene "in individual cases" (*in singulis casibus*) is unquestionable, even if there was no mention of it in Art. 9 of the *Decree.* Some think that this right is ineffective if the Orientals are not legally obliged to consult the Holy See about candidates to the episcopate. This is not so. As always in the past, the right to intervene would remain in full force even if the Holy Father should show his confidence in the Orientals by allowing them to elect their own bishops and to rule, in total liberty, in all other matters (*quaevis negotia*) of the patriarchate. Nor should there be fear that immutable primatial rights would lapse because unused. The Orientals, for their part, are fully conscious of the ecumenical necessity that they must do nothing which would diminish this confidence and force the Holy See to intervene more often than it did in the first thousand years of our era.

As regards the bibliography on the patriarchs and the autonomy of the Oriental Churches, some new items are listed in this section, which have appeared since my article in *Concilium* (Vol. 8, 1965).

E. Proposals for Unity and Diversity in Oriental Canon Law

In a short article in *Orientierung* for 1965, De Vries discusses certain principles of the *Decree* that denote a substantial and definite change of the West's attitude toward the Orientals. He

underlines three major issues (besides the patriarchal structure
of the Church) which will certainly have a great impact on any
future codification. First, the spiritual, liturgical, theological, historical, and disciplinary heritage of the Christian East is granted
its rightful place in the universal patrimony of the Church. The
Council *sollemniter declarat* the right and duty of the Oriental
Churches to govern themselves in accordance with their heritage
and recognizes and acknowledges that this is the best means of
bringing salvation to their faithful (Arts. 5-6). Secondly, the
Decree emphatically declares that the Universal Church is composed of particular Churches, of which the Latin or Western
Church, though numerically the strongest, is but one (Arts. 2
and 3). The Council rejects the formerly widespread conceptions that the Catholic and Latin Church are synonymous and
that the Latin Church enjoys a *praestantia* over the Oriental
Churches. Thirdly, since the diversity in non-essential matters
is accounted as a precious value in itself (Art. 2), there follows
the necessity of distinguishing clearly between what is essential
and what is accidental in the Church's patrimony and of foster-
ing both unity and diversity in Catholic theology, spirituality,
and discipline.

In a speech to the Commission for the Revision of *Codex
iuris canonici* on November 20, 1965, Pope Paul VI proposed
the question whether two different Codes should be compiled,
one for the West, the other for the East; or a single universal
Code that would contain all the constitutional law of the Church.
The solution of this "great problem" depends, to a large extent,
on how one understands the three principles mentioned above.
In fact, they may be reduced to a single one: each Oriental
Church has as much right as the Latin Church for a special
Code, because each Church is obliged to preserve her heritage
and to utilize it as the best means for the salvation of her faithful.

In an article in *Concilium* (Vol. 8, 1965) Huizing presents
a bibliographical survey on the Constitutional Law of the Church.
Among others, he mentions Breydy. In 1961 this author proposed that there should exist, for ecumenical reasons, a single

Constitutional Law for the whole Church with individual Codes for the Latin Church, the Oriental Church, new Churches etc. Like many others, Breydy did not perceive at that time that "a Code for the Oriental Church" would run counter to the three principles mentioned above.

Since this volume of *Concilium* includes an article by Bishop N. Edelby on why there should be a separate codification for the Oriental and Roman Churches, a few words will suffice for what the Orientals regard as the "great problem". It seems that they generally agree on the need for two codifications. However, some, like Bishop Ziadeh and Bishop Doumith, have written on the necessity of a "single Code in the Church"; yet, what they actually propose is a Constitution with as many Codes as there are Churches. Both are averse to the present Oriental Code not because it is distinct from the Latin one, but because it fails to differentiate between the individual Oriental Churches. They believe that the present Code because it is "apparently Byzantine, but really Latin in spirit", disregards the genuine traditions of the non-Byzantine Churches; that is, of the Armenians, Copts, Ethiopians, Chaldeans, Maronites, Malabarese, and Malankarese. Bishop Ziadeh affirms that he rejects "two Codes" precisely because of his twofold concern for the non-Latinization (and non-Byzantinization of some Churches) and for the future reunion with the separated Churches. To plead for a single basic Code, he says, is to ask for unity in diversity. However, when he makes specific proposals, in his article in *Antiochena* (n. 8), he seems to be opting for something closer to the present *Codex iuris canonici* than for a Constitutional Law of the Church. Bishop Doumith goes farther. He refuses to accept a dualistic conception of the Church (East and West). Such an outlook he considers anachronistic, objectively unfounded and theologically erroneous. For him the Church should not be divided into East and West, but according to particular Churches, "patriarchates", because these still best correspond to the present-day ethnical and cultural situation in what is geographically called "East". According to Doumith's conceptions the Constitutional Law of the Church should embrace only those fundamental laws, without which unity is impossible: *in necessariis unitas*. Outside of this, each Church should be left free to draw up its own Code. After reading Doumith's article one would conclude that a Constitutional Law, as he conceives it, would be the best means to foster the ecumenical dialogue; for it would save the relative autonomy of all Oriental Churches, allay any fear of Latinization or Byzantinization, and, in fact, do away with the discrimination between East and West. McGrath (p. 459) also desires a Constitutional Law for the following reasons: "(a) The unity of the People of God in the Holy Spirit would shine forth. (b) The diversity found in various Churches would be accepted for what it is: the result of the inspiration of divine providence. (c) The ecumenical spirit of Vatican Council II would be furthered by the proclamation of unity in essentials, freedom in accidentals, and charity in all things."

To the above principles another important one should be added. The *Decree* counsels prelates of the various individual Churches, especially those having jurisdiction in the same territory, to foster unity of action (Art. 4). Thus the hierarchies of each Church should strive for unity at least in such practical matters as the laws which invalidate juridical acts; e.g., the laws on marriage impediments.

F. SOME REMARKS ON THE LITERATURE ON ORIENTAL CANON LAW

This author has published an almost complete bibliography on this subject in *Concilium*, Vol. 8, 1965, and in *Periodica de re morali-canonica-liturgica* of 1966 (285-289), where the recent literature on the *Decree on the Catholic Oriental Churches* may be found. The present article brings the bibliography further up to date.

Commentaries on the *Decree* have been written by members of the Preparatory Commission for the *Decree* (Hoeck, Wojnar,

Pujol) and by other outstanding experts in Oriental matters (De Vries, Pospishil). In a very objective and ecumenically minded commentary, Hoeck reveals how the texts varied in different schemata of the *Decree*. Wojnar, Pospishil and Pujol have commented on the *Decree* from a canonical viewpoint. Among other works mention should be made of Esposito and Sotomayor. The latter has employed best of all the various speeches that were made in the Council. For the history of the *Decree*, Caprile's article should be consulted. Of about 20 other authors who have commented in one way or other on the *Decree*, one feels obliged to single out De Vries, Diez, O'Connel, Mahfoud and Stakemeier. It should be noted, however, that a truly scientific commentary cannot be written until the *modi* and other key documents kept in the Vatican archives are released.

At the 138th session of the Council Zoghby raised the question of the indissolubility of marriage. Cardinal Journet, Crouzel, Wenger, Dauvillier, Dubarle, Martinez and others have recently subjected the matter to close scrutiny. Kerame re-echoes Zoghby's position in an article to which the editors have added three very interesting appendices. Poisson focuses the whole problem in a short but perceptive article in a Canadian review. Zoghby's views were not accepted for discussion in the Council because they were considered to be opposed to Catholic doctrine and were officially declared by Patriarch Maximos IV to be private opinions that do not reflect the mind of the Melchite Church. In a document of November, 1966, however, the patriarch pleaded for a commission to study whether some remedy might be found for those who, through no fault of their own, were abandoned by their spouses and subsequently attempted a second marriage.

The question of the indissolubility of marriage will certainly be a main topic of discussion in any ecumenical meeting. It will center on the difference between a sacramental non-consummated marriage and a consummated one. The Orthodox insist on the sacramental character of Christian marriage, but fail to see how consummation so solidifies the sacramental bond that not even the vicarial power of the pope can dissolve it. For one, Christofilopoulos (p. 242) denies that consummation has any sacramental significance.

As regards the question of *communicatio in sacris,* it is pleasant to note the favorable response that Uržumcev in the *Moscow Patriarchal Review* makes to Cardinal Bea's article on the significance of the eucharist for Christian union. In the United States, however, the Conference of Orthodox Bishops, in a meeting on January 22, 1965, vigorously rejected any (also exceptional) common participation in the eucharist. An article in *The Word,* a Syrian Orthodox review, also sharply rejects the possibility of such a *communicatio.* In the *Eastern Churches Review* Archbishop Anthony refuses to countenance any *communicatio* in the eucharist, but expresses himself in very mild terms. The Catholic hierarchies have issued many rulings on the *communicatio,* but that of Cardinal Slipyj seems to be most far-reaching, mainly because of the peculiar conditions affecting his 5 million subjects in the U.S.S.R. What the future canons on *communicatio in sacris* will look like may be seen in a recent article by Risk.

Finally, it is worth noting that, despite the common declaration of Pope Paul VI and the Ecumenical Patriarch Athenagoras of December 7, 1965, on the "consignment to oblivion" of the anathemas of 1054, the canonical separation between the two Churches still exists. Scrima (p. 25) affirms that "it would be particularly incorrect to see in it an invitation to sacramental intercommunion" since a "full communion in sacramental life presupposes . . . full realization of the common apostolic faith".

BIBLIOGRAPHY

A. The Commission for the Oriental Code

The best information with ample bibliography about this Commission may be found in *Oriente Cattolico,* Vatican City, 1962, 35-61, and in two articles by D. Faltin (the Assistant of the Commission) published in

Dictionarium morale et canonicum (*cura Petri Palazzini*) Rome, Vol. I, 1962, "Codex iuris canonici orientalis", 719-722, and Vol. III, 1966, "Legislatio latino-orientalis", 33-36. For the actual composition of the Pontifical Commissions, *cf. Annuario Pontificio,* 1966, 1002-1005.

B. A Provisional and Ecumenical Codification for the "Uniate Churches"

The *Memorandum* of the Orthodox observers is printed in Greek in *Pantainos* 56(1964)489-492.

R. MURRAY, 'The Orthodox and Reunion', *The Month,* January, 1967, 18-26.

C.-J. DUMOND, 'La troisième conférence pan-orthodoxe', *Vers l'unité chrétienne* 17(1964), Sept.-Nov., 73-80.

J. AUCAGNE, 'Oecuménisme et Orient Chrétien', *Études,* 1965, May, 707-723.

L. VISCHER, 'Nach der dritten Session des Zweiten Vatikanischen Konzils', *Ökumenische Rundschau* 14(1965)97-116.

Msgr. CHRYSOSTOMOS: 'Mgr. Chrysostomos nous parle de l'avenir des Églises unies à Rome', *Informations Catholiques Internationales,* 1966, no.256, 5-6: 'Les Églises unies dans le dialogue oecuménique', *ibidem,* no. 278, 26-27.

Msgr. E. ZOGHBY, 'Les Églises unies dans le dialogue avec l'Orthodoxie', *ibidem,* no. 267, 28-30.

Antiochena no. 12, 1966, 'Le devenir des Uniates: Réflexions sur deux interviews' (Mgr. Chrysostomos- Mgr. Zoghby).

J. HOECK, 'Dekret über die Katholischen Ostkirchen', edited in Herder's *Das Zweite Vatikanische Konzil,* 1965, 362-392.

C. The Non-Binding Character of the Code for the Orthodox and the Recognition of Their Jurisdiction

P. HUIZING, 'Should the Ecclesiastical Marriage Laws be revised?', *Concilium* (English edition), 1966, October, Vol. 8, no. 2, 82-88.

I. ŽUŽEK, 'Animadversiones quaedam in Decretum de ecclesiis orientalibus catholicis Concilii Vaticani II', *Periodica de re morali-canonica-liturgica* 55(1966) 266-288.

A. COUSSA, *Epitome praelectionum de iure ecclesiastico orientali,* vol. I, 1948, Rome, nos. 15-21.

E. HERMAN, 'Quibus legibus subiiciantur Dissidentes rituum orientalium', *Il Diritto Ecclesiastico* 62(1951)1043-1058.

D. FALTIN, 'De legibus quibus Orientales acatholici ritui orientali adscripti tenentur', *Apollinaris* 35(1962)238-249.

C. PUJOL, 'Orientales ab Ecclesia Catholica seiuncti teneturne novo iure canonico a Pio XII promulgato?', *Orientalia Christiana Periodica* 32(1966)78-110.

W. BERTRAMS, 'De gradibus "Communionis" in doctrina Concilii Vaticani II', *Gregorianum* 47(1966)286-305.

W. DE VRIES, *Rom und die Patriarchate des Ostens*, Freiburg-München, 1963; 'I Patriarcati separati d'Oriente nella concezione della S. Sede', *Unitas* (Italian edition) 18(1963)105-123.

D. PATRIARCHAL RIGHTS AND THE "AUTONOMY"
OF CHURCHES IN ORIENTAL CANON LAW

J. HOECK: *cf.* under B.

V. POSPISHIL, *Orientalium Ecclesiarum: The Decree on the Eastern Catholic Churches of the II Council of Vatican*, New York, 1965.

M. WOJNAR, 'Decree on the Oriental Catholic Churches', *The Jurist* 25(1965)173-203.

I. ŽUŽEK: *cf.* under C.

L'Église Grecque Melkite au Concile: Discours et notes du Patriarche Maximos IV et des Prélats de son Église au Concile Oecuménique Vatican II, Beyrouth, 1967.

Some Recent Works on the Patriarchs and the "Autonomy" of Oriental Churches:

M. CONSTANDACHE, 'Patriarhia si demnitatea de patriarch in Biserica Ortodoxă' ('Le Patriarcat et la dignité de patriarche dans l'Église Orthodoxe'), *Ortodoxia* 17(1965)225-249.

J. HAJJAR, 'Les Synodes dans l'Église orientale', *Concilium* (English editon), 1965, no.8,30-34.

C. DE CLERCQ, 'Initia iuridica Ecclesiarum Orientalium', *Apollinaris* 38(1965)215-235; 'Diversitas iuridica Ecclesiarum Orientalium', *ibidem* pp.348-371.

W. DE VRIES, 'The College of Patriarchs', *Concilium* 35-44. (English edition, no.8,1965.

J. MOUNAYER, *Les synodes syriens Jacobites*, Beyrouth, 1964.

E. MARINA, 'Temeiuri istorice și canonice ale sinodului permanent' ('Les bases historiques et canoniques du synode permanent'), *Studii Teologice* 18(1966)190-214; 'Episcopii ajutători și episcopii vicari', ('Les évêques adjoints et les vicaires'), *ibidem* 17(1965)418-440.

V. POSPISHIL, *Der Patriarch in der Serbisch-Orthodoxen Kirche*, Wien, 1966.

A. LAMPART, *Ein Märtyrer der Union mit Rom, Joseph I. (1681-1696) Patriarch der Chaldäer*, Einsiedeln, 1966.

Unpublished dissertations:

M. BROGI, *Il Patriarca nelle Fonti Giuridiche della Chiesa Copta,* Rome (Pont. Oriental Institute), 1966.

C. MALANCHARUVIL, *The Syro-Malankara Church: Its Juridical Status,* Rome (Gregorian University), 1965.

G. PADINJAREKUTT, *Appointment of Bishops in the Chaldean Church,* Rome (Pont. Oriental Institute), 1967.

E. Proposals for Unity and Diversity in Oriental Canon Law

W. DE VRIES, 'Das Konzilsdekret über die katholischen orientalischen Kirchen', *Orientierung* 29(1965) 201-204.

P. HUIZING, 'The Reform of Canon Law', *Concilium,* 1965, no. 8.

M. BREYDY, 'Diálogo canónico entre orientales y occidentales', *Estudios de Deusto* 9(1961)140-150.

Msgr. I. ZIADEH, 'Sur la nécessité d'un unique code de droit canonique pour l'Église', *Antiochena,* 1965, no. 6, 11-14; the English translation of this article is in *One in Christ* 2(1966)70-74. The same article, somewhat enlarged, appeared also in *L'Orient Syrien* 11(1966)90-98. A complementary note is published in *Antiochena,* 1965, no. 8, 23-24.

Msgr. M. DOUMITH, 'De l'unité du Code de droit dans l'Église Catholique', *Antiochena,* 1965, no. 7, pp. 23-27.

J. McGRATH, 'Canon Law for the Church and the Churches', *The Jurist* 26(1966)454-459.

F. Some Remarks on the Literature on Oriental Canon Law

I. ŽUŽEK, 'Oriental Canon Law: Survey of Recent Developments', *Concilium,* 1965, no. 8: for the article in *Periodica* . . . *cf.* under C.

J. HOECK: *cf.* under B.

M. WOJNAR: *cf.* under D.

C. PUJOL, 'Decreto conciliare sulle Chiese Orientali Cattoliche', *Unitas* (Italian edition) 17(1965) 167-181. The best commentary by Pujol is being prepared at present for publication by *Ediciones Fax,* Madrid. I wish to express here my gratitude for the use of the manuscript.

W. DE VRIES, 'Il decreto conciliare sulle Chiese Orientali Cattoliche', *La Civiltà Cattolica* 116 (17 April 1965), no. 2756, 106-121: for the article in *Orientierung cf.* under E.

V. POSPISHIL: *cf.* under D.

R. ESPOSITO, *Il Decreto conciliare sulle Chiese Orientali 'Orientalium Ecclesiarum'*, Rome, 1965.

M. SOTOMAYOR, *Decreto sobre las Iglesias Orientales Católicas* Madrid, 1965.

G. CAPRILE: *cf.* 'Lavori del concilio', *La Civiltà Cattolica* 116 (20 March 1965), vol. 2754, 578-599.

L. DIEZ, 'El Decreto conciliar sobre las Iglesias Orientales Católicas', *Re-Unión* 106(1965)315-337.

P. O'CONNEL, *The Decree on the Catholic Eastern Churches*, Dublin, 1965.

P. MAHFOUD, 'Quel rite doit adopter le fidèle oriental acatholique qui rejoint l'Église catholique', *Apollinaris* 38(1965)175-185 (on art. 4 of the *Decree*); 'Les mariages mixtes', *ibidem*, 84-95; 'Les mariages mixtes: Problème de licéité en droit canonique oriental actuel', *ibidem* 39(1966)71-92 (on art. 18 of the *Decree*).

E. STAKEMEIER, 'Erläuterungen zum Dekret Über die Katholischen Orientalischen Kirchen', *Catholica* 19(1965)72-82. 'Das Konzilsdekret über die Katholischen Orientalischen Kirchen, *ibidem*, 254-261.

Msgr. E. ZOGHBY's interventions in the Council on the indissolubility of marriage and the relative documents of the Patriarch MAXIMOS IV are best published in *L'Église Grecque Melkite au Concile*, Beyrouth, 1967, 463-470.

Card. Ch. JOURNET, 'Le marriage indissoluble', *Nova et Vetera*, 1966, no. 1, and in *La Documentation Catholique* 63 (1966), no. 1473, col. 1075-1094.

H. CROUZEL, 'Séparation ou remariage selon les Pères anciens', *Gregorianum* 47(1966)472-494.

A. WENGER, *Vatican II, chronique de la quatrième session*, Paris, 1966, 200-246.

J. DAUVILLIER, 'L'indissolubilité du mariage dans la nouvelle loi', *L'Orient Syrien* 9(1964)265-290.

A. DUBARLE, 'Mariage et divorce dans l'Évangile', *L'Orient Syrien* 9(1964)61-73; *cf.* a short note of the author in *Revue des Sciences philosophiques et théologiques* 50(1966)599-600.

G. MARTÍNEZ, 'Indisolubilidad del matrimonio rato y consumado entre dos partes bautizadas', *Revista Española de Derecho Canónico* 20(1965)481-523.

O. KERAME, 'Oecuménisme et indissolubilité du mariage', *Le Lien* 31(1966), no. 1., 19-24: with 3 Appendices, 25-28.

G. POISSON, 'Une question actuelle: l'indissolubilité du mariage', *Monde Nouveau* 27(1966), no. 3 March, 83-87.

A. CHRISTOFILOPOULOS, *Hellenikon ekklesiastikon dikaion*, Athens, ('Cardinal A. Bea on the Eucharist and the Unity of Christians'),

P. URŽUMCEV, 'Kardinal Avgustin Bea o Evcharistii i edinstve Christian' 1965.
Žurnal Moskovskoj Patriarchii, 1966, no. 2, 55-58.

Card. A. BEA, 'L'Eucaristia e l'unione dei cristiani', *La Civiltà Cattolica* 116 (4 September 1965), vol. 2765, 401-413.

For the decision of the Conference of the Orthodox Bishops of America cf. *St. Vladimir's Seminary Quarterly* 9(1965)38 and *Ostkirchliche Studien* 14(1965)201-202.

The Word 9(1965), no. 2, 6 and 8: 'Orthodox and Catholic Intercommunion'.

Archbishop ANTHONY, 'Vatican II and the Eastern Churches', a comment in *Eastern Churches Review* 1(1966)19-21.

Card. J. SLIPYJ's decree on the *communicatio in sacris* is printed in *Blagovisnik* . . . or *Litterae-Nuntiae Archiepiscopi Maioris* . . . 2(1966)45-46.

J. RISK, 'De reformandis canonibus qui regulant communicationem in sacris', *Periodica de re morali-canonica-liturgica* 55(1966)694-724.

A. SCRIMA, 'The Lifting of the Anathemas', *Eastern Churches Review* 1(1966)23-26.

PART III
DOCUMENTATION
CONCILIUM

Office of the Executive Secretary
Nijmegen, Netherlands

PART III

Concilium General Secretariat/*Nijmegen, Netherlands*

Stirrings in Religious Life

" Remember not the former things, nor consider the things of old. Behold, I am doing a new thing; now it springs forth, do you not perceive it?" (Is. 43, 18-19).[1]

With Vatican Council II the whole Church began to stir, and it is therefore hardly astonishing that religious life, too, does no longer present that static appearance to which we were accustomed. Both in theory and in practice it has gone a new way which differs from that of a decade ago.[2] Are these stirrings the last convulsions of an approaching agony or the signs of a new life? It is not enough to judge this question on a merely subjective optimism or pessimism. Therefore, we have tried to provide here a responsible survey of those stirrings which have attracted

[1] We gratefully acknowledge the assistance given at a colloquy in which the following took part: Dr. Lydia Simons, Prof. Drs. A. van Galen, O.C., Dom A. Nuy, O.S.B., Prof. Drs. A. van Rijen, M.S.C., Prof. Dr. P. Smulders, S.J. and a team from the General Secretariat; for a discussion of the origin of the conciliar documents on religious life and a detailed commentary, cf. J. M. R. Tillard, *L'adaptation et la rénovation de la vie religieuse* (Unam Sanctam, 62) (Paris, 1967); *Dekret über die zeitgemäsze Erneuerung des Ordenslebens mit den Ausführungsbestimmungen Lateinish und Deutsch*, with introductions by F. Wulf (Münster, 1967).

[2] For a scientific survey of this development, see Dom R. Lemoine, O.S.B., *Le droit des religieux du Concile de Trente aux Instituts séculiers. Evolution historique du droit des religieux*, with a preface by Gabriel Le Bras (Bruges/Paris, 1955).

the attention of theologians in recent publications and which are not limited to local phenomena.

A first overall impression of such a survey is that religious life shows more optimism in Protestantism than in contemporary Catholicism. This difference can be explained for a large part by the difference in theological attitude taken up by the Reformation and the Catholic Church toward religious life since the Council of Trent. While the Reformation rejected religious life as one of the clearest expressions of justification by works and of unfaithfulness to the God-given mission of creation, the Counter-Reformation emphasized religious life as the state of perfection,[3] as a kind of spiritual aristocracy. Both sides have corrected this one-sidedness. Sometimes this change is so explicit that the outsider has the impression that Protestantism shows more enthusiasm for religious life than Catholicism. A closer look, however, shows that Catholic skepticism about pre-conciliar religious life derives from a justified dissatisfaction with a juridical approach and institutionalization that no longer appeal to our modern sense of living. Protestant enthusiasm then appears to derive from the fact that Protestants are not yet confronted with an ideological burden and can start without the disadvantage of a backwash of historical wear-and-tear.

It should also be noted that the numerically small number of religious in Protestant and Anglican Churches is felt rather as a remnant of "high Church" tendencies than as something touching the heart of the Church itself. Catholic theology sees this life rather as an essential expression of the Church as such.

We shall first give a brief survey of the Protestant explanation of these rather recent forms of religious life. We shall then proceed to deal with the main points of Catholic dissatisfaction with actual religious life, indicate the background for the present skep-

---

[3] This one-sided approach in Protestantism has been best expressed by A. Harnack, in *Das Mönchtum, Seine Ideale und Seine Geschichte* (Giessen, [5]1900); for the origin of religious life, cf. P. Festugière, *Les moines d'Orient* I (Paris, 1959); J. Peters, "Naar een theologie van de Evangelische Raden," in *Jaarboek 1963/4 Werkgenootschap van katholieke Theologen in Nederland* (Hilversum, 1965), pp. 169-93.

tical attitude toward institutionalized religious life and show how this critical skepticism may lead to a renewal of religious life in the Catholic Church.

I

THE PROTESTANT EXPLANATION OF RELIGIOUS LIFE

There is not much sense in the glib assertion that religious life in the Catholic Church is declining while it experiences a new flowering in Protestantism. The crisis simply has come earlier for Catholics and there are signs that the relatively recent religious communities of Protestantism[4] may soon have to face it, too, as is clear from the fact that these movements are only recognized by Calvinism and the Lutheran high Church. To assess a numerically limited phenomenon such as a new appreciation of religious life in a specific movement within Calvinistic theology one cannot forget that a similar re-appreciation took place in Catholicism already at the end of the 19th century (the Dominicans under Lacordaire, Guéranger and the liturgical movement of Solesmes, the Paulist Fathers in the United States, Newman and the Oratory in England). Seen in this perspective the Protestant movement rather appears to be a belated flowering after the harvest than the first flowering of an approaching spring. Such a critical assessment is the more necessary when there is danger of thinking too soon that there is enough common ground to start building up an ecumenical inter-Church religious life. As L. Dingemans[5] observed at the ecumenical study days of

---

[4] For a survey of Protestant religious institutions, cf. Lydia Prager, *Frei für Gott und die Menschen—Evangelische Bruder- und Schwesterschaften der Gegenwart in Selbstdarstellungen* (Stuttgart, [2]1964); for the theological justification of Taizé, see R. Schütz, *Living Today for God* (Baltimore, 1962); "The Taizé Vocation," in *Theology* 565 (July, 1967), pp. 309-15; *idem, Unity, Man's Tomorrow* (London, 1962).

[5] These study days were held from April 3-8, 1967, in the Institut Saint André (Belgium). In 1965 and 1966 Anglican and Catholic religious met in the United States. In Ramegnies-Chin there was a gathering of 120 Anglican, Catholic, Orthodox and Protestant religious. The way in which G. Trifitt, superior general of the Anglican Society of St. John

Ramegnies-Chin, the situation is influenced by sociological factors of which we are as yet only half aware. Religious life is not a purely Christian phenomenon; other great religions, too, show religious groups with a social structure that is very similar to that of Christian communities. We shall return to this point in the second part of this article where we shall deal with the link between secularization and religious life. For the moment we want to limit the discussion to the ecclesiological aspect of the Calvinist re-assessment of religious life.

The re-discovery of the Church, particularly as mystery in a theology like that of Karl Barth, shows a curious correspondence with the rise of a religious life which sees itself as an intensification of that ecclesiological reality. Particularly in Taizé, the paradoxical existence of which has been most clearly explained theologically by R. Schütz and Max Thurian, this close connection between ecclesiology and religious life is most prominent.[6] The Brothers of Taizé consider that there are two types of Christian community life in the New Testament. The first type is that of the symbolic community: closed, limited, based on the model of the apostolic college with life and property in common. This type they call the Jerusalem community. The second type is the community which is outward-going to the world: the ordinary ecclesiastical community, which they call the Pauline community. They consider both types necessary for a healthy communal life. The Jerusalem type they see as perpetuated in the monastic orders. This type, however, has been constantly pushed into the background, to the detriment of the (Protestant) Churches. That is why they consider it a special *vocation* to represent the Jerusalem type today.

Evangelist, stressed unity of experience is too one-sided and pietistic as an approach to the more complex problem of Christian unity; it is a too extreme contrast between theology and spirituality. A spirituality which does not rest on a sound theology (which does not prevent it from correcting theology) becomes too easily fanatical, and there is nothing more dangerous for genuine unity.

[6] R. Schütz, *La Règle de Taizé* (Taizé, 1954); C. van de Loo, "Kloosterorden in het reformatorisch christendom," in *Streven* XIV (Aug.-Sept., 1961), pp. 1104-9.

In all this, Taizé differs essentially from, for example, the German *Michaelbruderschaft* (the fraternity of St. Michael), who see their work as a service of representation and an avant-garde movement. They start from the principle that all Church members really ought to do what the fraternity is provisionally doing for them in a representative character. Taizé maintains, however, explicitly that not all should act as they do: this demands a special vocation. But this vocation is of no higher value than that of the Pauline community member: both are necessary. It concerns here not so much a community already existing as an institution, but rather the creativity that constantly gives rise to community life in a new manner, as it springs from the working out of the personal vocation and faith in the Gospel. This is perhaps one of the reasons why Taizé can bring so many Protestant communities into its community: the total of seventy members covers some twenty Churches. Religious experience (the pietistic element) and the celebration of the eucharist are also seen primarily as a community-building force. There is a deliberate attempt to break through every form of individualism in this search for new forms of community life. Such a community is definitely not seen as a community for usefulness or for the sake of mere activity. It is not a means toward something else, but the spiritual reality itself: the community is itself a realized aspect of salvation.[7]

Taizé frankly admits its debt to the great Catholic religious orders. This explains perhaps why it so easily appeals to the Catholic at first contact: he recognizes there something that he would like very much to see as an ideal in his own Church, a genuine synthesis of action and contemplation and whatever is of value in the various spiritualities that are claimed as a privilege by the various orders in the Church of Rome. He will have to ask himself, though, whether he is more charmed by what is new than by the vision of a style of religious life which has meaning for the future. He should beware of new myths. A closer

[7] J. Murphy-O'Connor, "Péché et communauté dans le Nouveau Testament," in *Rev. Bibl.* 64 (April, 1967), pp. 161-93.

look reveals that these communities, too, have the difficulty of passing from the original inspiration to the second generation. The history of Catholic religious life shows that this difficulty is almost insurmountable: the second generation almost always institutionalizes. This inevitably leads to a loss of the original freshness, but frequently it goes further and the real inspiration which led to religious creativity is pushed in a direction that differs from what the prophetic founder intended.

This critical observation about movements such as that of Taizé does not mean to deny that these religious communities can function as a sign of hope for religious life at large, but merely points out that they provide no solution for the critical situation of religious life in the Catholic Church. The obvious esteem that these numerically small but qualitatively influential religious communities enjoy in some Protestant Churches cannot be repeated in the Catholic Church because of the historical situation.[8] Here one touches a definite psychological dissatisfaction with institutionalized religious life itself. We shall try to give a broad analysis of this feeling of dissatisfaction and then survey the critical situation and what is being done among Catholics to bring about a renewal.

II
THE CRISIS IN THE CATHOLIC THEOLOGY OF RELIGIOUS LIFE

The dissatisfaction of the religious themselves with the institutionalization of religious life does not concern only one or other aspect: it is general. The younger members maintain that they do not find what they were looking for while the older ones treat

---

[8] P. Philippi, "Bruderschaften zwischen Gemeinde und Amt," in *Geschichtswirklichkeit und Glaubensbewährung* (Stuttgart, 1967), pp. 310-1; cf. K. Barth, *Dogmatik* III (Zürich, 1957), pp. 4, 137 and 164: "There is a genuine Christian value which does not lead man to marriage but beyond it." According to Barth, therefore, one should not "so glibly pass it over as up till now has been the case".

the traditional foundation of religious life as an ideology. It is not so much a matter of laxity in observance or of the collapse of enthusiasm for contemplative life in particular over the last ten years. It is rather a matter of the absence of a vision for the future. The institution gives the impression that one is so tied up with a world that belongs to the past that it prevents people from being seriously committed to the world of the future. People are asked to be totally committed to something that they doubt the value of for the future.[9] This general dissatisfaction has still deeper causes that most religious cannot pin down to definite formulae. The value of religious life as it is, is no longer self-evident and courageous efforts are being made to discover the real meaning.

A vast and frequently repetitive literature gives the impression that one is trying to restore or prop up the weak spots in a centuries-old castle, still imposing enough to convey the greatness of a past culture. As the damage is assessed some even speak of completely rebuilding it.[10] Occasionally Taizé is envied for not being weighed down by the burden of history. Yet, gradually the awareness of this passage of history shows up the fact that religious life itself is subject to this law of history, and this is a positive gain. One gets nowhere with either naive optimism or total rejection. The best way of understanding the critical attitude of Catholic authors and their search for an effective, theologically justified renewal is perhaps to look at the points that stand out in their argument:

1. the strong secularizing tendency in present-day theology which seems to make religious life a form of alienation;

2. a better insight in the sociological conditions and factors of community building;

3. the new understanding brought about by anthropology;

[9] J. M. Delor, "La vie religieuse, signe lisible pour le monde d'aujourd'-hui," in *Rev. Dioc. Tournai* 21 (1966), pp. 382-94.

[10] J. Leclercq, "Le monachisme contesté," in *N. R. Th.* 89 (June, 1967), pp. 608-10. In this connection see the excellent series *Problèmes de vie religieuse,* and for this aspect especially n. 20, *Les religieux aujourd'hui et demain* (Paris, 1964) and n. 22 *Le mépris du monde* (Paris, 1965).

4. the discovery of the psychological factors that lie behind the classical formulation of the evangelical counsels;

5. the changes that have come over our ecclesiology;

6. the clericalization of the religious orders;

7. a certain dissatisfaction with the results of Vatican Council II in regard to religious life;

8. dissatisfaction with the levelling down and centralizing of religious life now that we understand better the historical process which brought it about.

1. The Secularizing Tendency in Present-Day Theology

"Secularizing tendency" means here that man today is aware of the fact that the fate of the world as well as his own destiny lies in his own hands, through science, technology and organization.[11] His cultural environment and education make him inclined to test every norm by its serviceability in the building up of a better human society.[12] This is why he tries to create new norms out of his own experience and the concrete world he lives in, hopefully steering toward an earthly future while fully realizing that it may turn out a failure. This fear does not, however, prevent him from reducing norms from outside or above to only relative values and renouncing a future above or outside this earth.

For a long time past religious life has been marked by a two-fold tendency: a withdrawal from the world and the desire for a new world, a dissatisfaction with the world as one finds it and the hope of a new world which it is thought one can help to build up. The present attempts at adaptation overstress perhaps the negative aspect of a flight from the world and underrate the positive aspect of a desire for a new world. The studies of Bultot in the "contempt of the world"[13] should help us to realize that

[11] Commissie van XVII, *Veranderingen in het religieuze leven en de achtergronden hiervan; idem, De geculariseerde wereld en het religieuze leven* (Nijmegen, 1967).

[12] R. Spiazzi, O.P., *Lo spirito e la regola di San Domenico* (Rome, 1967), p. 12.

[13] R. Bultot, "Anthropologie et spiritualité," in *Rev. Sc. Ph. et Th.* 61

this flight from the world sprang from dissatisfaction with the world of a particular cultural condition. The positive element lay in the belief that another world was possible. Whenever this flight from the world developed into a passive attitude, as with the Quietists, or before them, with the Flagellants and even in the movement of the *Docta Ignorantia* ("wise ignorance"), the Church condemned it. Those who inspired religious life authentically, such as Benedict, Francis, Dominic, Ignatius and others, were always driven by the vision of a new world. When, as in our days, the awareness of the world becomes more all-embracing, it becomes clearer where this vision was hampered by limitation and illusion.

Religious prophets, even in our time, such as a Fr. Lebbe, are necessarily limited in their vision. Their vision of a new world is limited by their cultural environment, and this is inevitable. This limitation becomes dangerous only when the problems of such a vision and therefore the vision itself are universalized. This was still possible when the Western world was a cultural unit. With the discovery of the new world, and certainly with the expansion of missionary activity this attitude not only recoiled on the universal Church which began to universalize local problems but also on the religious movements that spread all over the world.[14]

Today we feel this problem still more strongly.[15] Religious, too, are susceptible to the somewhat vague demand for a new world.[16] In such circumstances the flight from the world is no longer acceptable and is rejected; it is even thought that only

---

(Jan. 1967), pp. 3-22; cf. the special issue of *Rev. d'Asc. et Myst.* 41 (1965).

[14] R. M. Tschidimbo, "La rénovation de la vie religieuse et les missions," in Tillard, *L'Adaptation et la rénovation* (Paris, 1967), pp. 525-40; L. Hughes, "Religious Renewal and the Mission," in *The Way* (May, 1966), pp. 108-12.

[15] E. Schillebeeckx, "Het nieuwe mens- en Godsbeeld in conflict met het religieuze leven" (Summary: The Religious Life in Conflict with the New Idea of God and Man), in *T. V. T.* 7 (Jan.-March, 1967), pp. 1-27.

[16] R. Rouquette, "Les Jésuites et la question sociale en Amérique latine," in *Etudes* (April, 1967), pp. 564-8.

now we can really begin to talk of the full value of religious life. The other tendency, the vision of a new world, gets bogged down too much in a superficial secularization tendency and gets too easily identified with an unqualified approach to that new world that has to be built. More recent publications[17] rather stress the pluriformity of the world: there are many worlds, and among them there is room for what may be called the religious world. The real crisis of religious life lies precisely in a lack of vision about the part the religious can play in the world of tomorrow. Their task might conceivably lie in a positive dissatisfaction with a too secular conception of that world of tomorrow; in the discovery of religious dimensions in that world, just as the world of artists will discover artistic dimensions in that technological world of tomorrow. Here and there[18] one reads about religious as a kind of evangelical free lances. What Käsemann pointed out as a defect in the whole of Christendom may well apply to the institutionalized world of religious life: "There are too many regular officers and too few partisans, yet only inspired partisans can haul the Church out of the ghetto of an out-of-date Christian culture."

The concern with earthly values, which occupies the religious horizon, certainly in the West, so completely that it threatens to blind us to other dimensions, certainly does not make it any easier to value the evangelical counsels in their traditional form. An ethically justified act of renouncement, of denial, is only possible where the value of the object of renouncement is appreciated.[19] Worldly values and evangelical counsels are not two possibilities that compete with each other: both are necessary,

[17] P. Pernot, "Moines de l'an 1000 ou moines de l'an 2000," in *Signes du Temps* 11 (1966), pp. 22-5.

[18] See the report of a panel discussion on female religious in the United States in *The Nat. Cath. Reporter* (Jan. 11, 1967), pp. 10-1. Also cf. J. Daniélou, "La place des religieux dans la structure de l'Eglise," in *L'Eglise du Vatican II* (Paris, 1966), pp. 1173-80; M. A. Neal, S.N.D., "Sociology and Community Change," in *The Changing Sister* (Notre Dame, 1965), p. 39.

[19] B. Delplanque, O.P., "La rénovation de la vie religieuse dans l'Eglise et le monde moderne," in *V.S.* 78 (1966), pp. 339-64.

and to choose one does not mean to reject the other. Evangelical counsels do not create a vacuum. Virginity learns also from marital love what love is and *vice versa;* poverty learns from economic labor the true ethical value of possession and without this economic labor, application and creativity, poverty is a mere sponging on the economic surplus of a welfare State. Without responsibility—also with regard to prophetic vision—and therefore without the readiness to suffer this responsibility, obedience is nothing but a lazy passivity and the repetition of religious and ecclesiastical behavior patterns that do not bring the future any closer. Without this sensitivity for earthly values, experienced as genuine values, the evangelical counsels lose their meaning in our time. On the other hand, love, autonomy and possession do not become fully operative in the Christian sense without the evident practice of the evangelical counsels. The unfolding of man's capacity to love also tends toward the love of God; man's desire for possession also tends to the possession of God (if we can only experience him as dispensable, he would not be real); the ability to listen, to accept elements from other cultures in our personal life (since this listening is the way in which we communicate with a world made "livable" by others) also tends toward a listening for sounds beyond the merely human ones. On these lines a genuine renewal of religious life can start as soon as one discovers, to quote Rahner,[20] that the evangelical counsels embody and manifest the faith in a grace of God that extends beyond this world.

2. *A Better Insight in the Sociological Conditions and Factors of Community Building*

When it is said that the religious community is a community of its own kind within the Church as a whole or that it is one of the various types of community building which a life based on the Gospel can produce, this community remains not only obscure but one cannot see clearly that it is subject to constant

[20] K. Rahner, "Ueber die evangelischen Räte," in *Geist und Leben* (Feb., 1964), p. 34 (*Schriften zur Theologie* VII [Einsiedeln, 1966], pp. 404-34).

change. To maintain a centuries-old framework and structures of authority obscures the authenticity of religious life. Sociology has taught us that these structures can be adjusted and therefore must be adjusted.[21] The non-Catholic L. Moulin praises the social legislation of the great orders and their ability to rejuvenate themselves.[22] Over against this there is the fact that a purely vertical system of authority makes any genuine community impossible. "A religious community which, through its structures, its breakdown in communication, its lack of human relationships and of elasticity in its environment, renders in practice the proper religious life of its members impossible or very difficult, releases them unilaterally from the bond it had accepted at the profession of its members (apart from the juridical implications)."[23] A religious community is also built through consultation and experiment, which does not exclude authority. Some authors have tried to find ethical norms for this experiment: the experimenting group should not be less than eight in number; it must not make it impossible for the community that is left behind to go on living; there must be a definite milieu for the life of the group while the milieu for its activities may vary without difficulty; one must have the courage to examine the motivation of the experiment scientifically; "in judging the particular form of the community the psychologist, the sociologist, the acting manager, the hygienic expert for the group, in short, the expert in community building must have the last word, and not the theologian".[24]

Here there is obviously also something that goes beyond these factors, although one should constantly beware of any glossing over structural faults through a mythical presentation from on

[21] R. Hostie et al., Menselijke verhoudingen in de communiteit (Bruges/Utrecht, 1967); J. H. Fichter, Religion as an occupation (Notre Dame, 1961); M. A. Baan, De Nederlandse minderbroedersprovincie sinds 1853. Sociologische verkeening van een religieuze groepering (Assen, 1965); V. Walgrave, Essai d'autocritique d'un ordre religieux. Les Dominicains en fin de Concile (Brussels, 1966).

[22] L. Moulin, Le monde vivant des religieux (Paris, 1964), p. 13: ". . . the secret of youth, long life, constant adjustment and constant renewal of the oldest political institutions of Europe."

[23] Schillebeeckx, op. cit., p. 21.

[24] Ibid., p. 24.

high. The general complaint that the institutional forms of religious life have become almost identical through direction from the center will then simply vanish.[25] Where there is a wish to establish smaller communities, it should be remembered that smaller numbers are not necessarily a guarantee of greater coziness. They will rather bring out more sharply the feeling of solitude. Solitude is as important to human life as mistakes and failures. There is solitude in "togetherness". The old adage of religious tradition, perhaps too romantically formulated as "blessed solitude", can have great value in contemporary ethics. It is an aspect that is brought out strongly today in a figure like Charles de Foucauld and in the spirituality of his *petits frères*.[26] These new forms are obviously closely linked with modern knowledge about man himself.

3. *The New Understanding Brought About by Anthropology*

This aspect of the demand for renewal may be expressed as follows: no longer is it enough to see religious life as something that is not harmful to the unfolding of man's possibilities; it must be seen as an authentic form of human life in its own right.

In principle, the question is here whether the religious form of life is a human form, while inspired by the Gospel. One may let oneself be inspired by the founder of the religious community to which one belongs or wants to belong, but more attention will be paid to the way in which such a prophetic person discovered a new form of human existence and service in the Gospel than to the actual concrete pattern of his own life.[27] A religious person will want to see his own life also as a process of growing self-awareness. It must be a growth that develops in the direction of God's presence in all that belongs to man's contemporary cultural achievements. The questions and doubts about religious life

[25] I. F. Goerres, "Mönch und Laie," in *Erbe und Auftrag* 42 (1966), p. 197.

[26] R. Voillaume, "La contemplation, élément essentiel de toute vie chrétienne," in Tillard, *L'adaptation*, etc., pp. 159-69.

[27] H. Carrier, "Sico-sociologia de la afiliación religiosa," in *Verbo divino* (Estella, 1965), p. 321.

arise from the personalist view of modern man and are lucidly summarized in the already quoted report of the Commission of XVII: "It is doubtful whether the present form of most religious communities leaves enough room for a harmonious unfolding of the human personality. It is not clear how the traditional concept of obedience can still fit in with the personalist view of man. Often the existing patterns of administration and authority do not correspond with the demand for personal responsibility and the decision of a personal conscience. The traditional religious formation and education did not sufficiently aim at the building up of free, responsible persons. The traditional spiritual and ascetic practices frequently derive from an antiquated dualistic view of man and his world. Among religious the emancipation of woman has not been given the same opportunities as in contemporary society." [28] We need, therefore, greater openness if meaningless isolation is not to lead to malformation. This concerns particularly the laws of enclosure.[29]

The religious wants to discover *how* he is necessary today: to say simply *that* he is necessary is unsatisfactory. He can only commit himself when he sees the possibility of making his own contribution within the context of his life. The characteristic feature of religious inspiration lies in the discovery of this ethical purpose of his life. This leads to a greater and deeper inwardness of religious life on all fronts: vocation, rule, constitution, structures, way of life, dress, and for this, a static way of life is inadequate.

The search for a specifically religious way of life, stimulated by contemporary anthropology, presents the problem of freedom also in a new light. It is not a matter of freedom *tout court* but of a freedom to create an atmosphere within which God's Word can be heard in a new tonality without thereby losing solidarity with the rest. In the practice of the evangelical counsels, too, the religious is learning to think about the relative freedom at his disposal.

[28] *Loc cit.*, p. 3.
[29] G. Tillmans, "Naar een dynamische opvatting van het slot der monialen," in *T.G.L.* (1967), pp. 183-95.

4. *The Discovery of the Psychological Factors that Lie behind the Classical Formulation of the Evangelical Counsels*

Yet, only 20 years ago religious life could be described as an "angelic" life. Though we can understand how this description came about historically in our tradition, the evangelical invitation to virginity is seen today as founded also on the human elements of such a pattern of life.[30] In a previous article in *Concilium,* it was already pointed out that the gospels contain more invitations to a closer following of Jesus than those contained in the three classical evangelical counsels. The renewal of religious life does not aim at a substitution or extension of these three counsels. We are simply faced with the fact that the institutionalized form in which the practice of these counsels has been fixed is no longer self-evident. One can talk as much as one likes about the symbolic value of these counsels, but they have lost much of this value through a host of circumstances. Occasionally, as in the case of obedience, these circumstances are linked with the petrifying rigidity which beset religious life after the Council of Trent.[31] Occasionally, as in the case of poverty, they find their explanation in the changed economic circumstances. Within this economic and "socialized" set-up of society one can comfortably renounce all property without thereby losing one's bread; at most, it hampers one's apostolic activity. If poverty is to remain a personal choice, it must be inspired by solidarity with man's material or spiritual needs. The real property of man in this productive society is his ability to produce and his talents. And these, even the religious cannot renounce. Poverty then will consist in putting one's talents at the service of the less fortunate; in not asserting oneself in spite of one's talents; in a certain clarification of purpose, *"transparence"*, as Taizé calls it; in productive service

---

[30] R. Vaughan, "Chastity and Psychosexual Development," in *Review for Religious* 23 (Nov., 1964), pp. 715-23; R. A. McCormick, "Psychosexual Development in Religious Life," *loc. cit.*, pp. 724-41.

[31] K. Rahner, "Eine ignatianische Grundhaltung. Marginalien zum Gehorsam," in *Stimmen der Zeit* 158 (1955/6), p. 253; A. Walsh, "A Note on Religious Maturity," in *The Way* 2 (May, 1966), pp. 113-9.

without looking for safety and security in possession;[32] in earning one's living, as is already being done in several experiments.

The loss of intelligibility in the matter of virginity has come about very much because of the new understanding of sex and the human body. Criticism is not, in the first place, aimed at the defects in the practice of virginity in earlier days, since marriage, too, is understood in a different way. It rather rests on the insight that, since Freud, the outsider can no longer see virginity as sheer generosity: it is also strongly influenced by psychological factors. The possibility of interpreting the vows in a merely negative manner, flight from responsibility, inability to be truly oneself through one's own creativity and not daring to commit oneself consciously in the field of sexual reality[33]—all this is too obvious today for us to expect that such a life can be appreciated as an obvious manifestation of "generosity". Thus, Taizé no longer values the evangelical counsels for their intrinsic greatness or excellence but as a means: this style of life makes man receptive to the message of the Gospel in another than usual way. The emphasis then falls on the word of the Gospel that "not everyone can see it".

Among Catholics the attempts at a renewal of the practice of the counsels in a more intelligible manner emphasize the humanist aspects of these counsels: they are a possible human way of life, although clearly differing from the usual. Is there then nothing specifically Christian in these counsels? Are they but mystifications of tasks that are beyond us? Not quite. They are a humanly possible pattern of life and at the same time this charismatic style of life, this existential inability to do or will otherwise, shows that such counsels as expressed, for instance, in the Sermon on the Mount, can in fact be put into practice. This is an essential

---

[32] K. Rahner, "Die Armut im Ordensleben in einer veränderten Welt," in *Geist und Leben* 33 (1960), p. 265; J. Giblet, "La joyeuse espérance des pauvres de Dieu," in *Anneau d'Or* 66 (1955), pp. 481-8.

[33] P. Ricoeur, *De l'interprétation: essai sur Freud* (Paris, 1965), pp. 520-9; M. Thurian, *Mariage et célibat* (Neuchâtel, 1964); J. Kerkhofs, "Aggiornamento van de religieuzen op wetenschappelijke basis," in *Streven* (Dec., 1965), pp. 242-8.

mission of the Church that has to proclaim the whole Gospel. The Church's secularity consists precisely in making the world habitable and livable also in this way. "One should not forget that if mankind would only develop in one direction the world would become practically uninhabitable: it would become the tyranny of an oligarchy of experts." [34] Of no single task of the Gospel can it be said *a priori* that it cannot be put into practice. One cannot measure the Gospel by some contemporary culture and then ask whether it contributes anything to this particular culture. Religious life is life in the present and in this culture, but it must be constantly subjected to evangelical criticism. What are called the inhuman imperatives of the Gospel could just as well be called pointers to unexpected possibilities in man. A particular style of life cannot always be immediately and consciously understood as a gain for the momentarily prevailing culture; it might, however, well show possible lines for future development. In this sense religious life will always have to be prophetic.

The durability of such a pattern of life should not be expressed in terms of temporal measurements, difficult to imagine (temporal vows, perpetual vows[35]), but in ethical terms of faithfulness. Precisely where a person remains faithful, also for psychological reasons, to a religious pattern of life, he becomes conscious of his specific limitation, but by the same token he creates the only human possibility of transcending it.

5. *The Changed Insights in Ecclesiology*

One may say that the idea of a uniform Church has been

[34] E. Schillebeeckx, *op. cit.*, p. 4.

[35] At the temporary profession one wonders what this means since it is a matter of a personal option and position; if the emphasis is put on the ethical aspect of loyalty it seems to exclude temporality; cf. H. F. Smith, "Temporary Religious Vocation," in *Review for Religious* 23 (July, 1964), pp. 433-44. For the three vows, see nn. 5, 6 and 7 of the series *Problèmes de vie religieuse: L'obéissance, La pauvreté* and *La Chasteté*. C. Pasquier, "Les besoins religieux des jeunes," in *La liberté évangélique* (Paris, 1965), pp. 210-1; A. van Rijen, "Het christelijk celibaat en zijn motivering," in *Ons Geestelijk Leven* 43 (1967), pp. 345-64.

overcome today. Even in the Middle Ages[36] religious life was felt to be another way of "being the Church" than the official one which was so closely intertwined with political structures. At the moment the pluriformity of the one Church is going to be asserted still more emphatically: "The one and only essential mission of the Church toward the world is to bear witness in the world, and this can be done in many ways and shapes, individually and collectively." [37] This has its repercussions on religious life. After Trent the organization of religious life in the various orders was a faithful copy of the hierarchical Church. Bernard already spoke of religious life in the paternalistically and feudally organized abbey as a kind of *ecclesiola in Ecclesia* (a little Church in the big one). Today's concept of religious life is not very happy with this description.[38] Religious life is now seen rather as another way of building the Church. In other words, the succession to the primitive Church runs through different layers; it is not merely a succession of bishops, but also a succession of charismata and of prophecy. With the rise of sociology it was already pointed out by Protestant authors[39] that it is curious how much similarity there is between Protestant sects and Catholic religious orders. Two types of religious grouping were distinguished: the "church" type and the "sect" type. The "sect" tends to be radical and an in-group: it tends to retain specific bits of the Gospel and to forge these fanatically into an abridged synthesis of the Gospel message which is in opposition to the world. The "church" is usually averse to this opposition between the world and the kingdom of God and tends to harmonize the demands of the Christian message with the realities

---

[36] J. Leclercq, *Initiation aux auteurs du Moyen Age: l'amour des lettres et le désir de Dieu* (Paris, 1957). This work is indispensable for an understanding of the theology of religious life.

[37] H. Küng, *Die Kirche* (Freiburg i. Br., 1967).

[38] Y. Congar underlines the dissenting opinion of Thomas: "Religious life is indeed a creation by the Church for her own end, which is the service of God as a social framework of life": *V.S.* 50, n. 3 (1959), p. 322.

[39] M. Weber, *Die protestantische Sekten und der Geist des Kapitalismus* (Tübingen, 1922), pp. 207-37; E. Troeltsch, *Die soziallehren der Christlichen Kirchen und Gruppen* I (Tübingen, 1920), p. 360.

and situations of this world. It is the type that addresses itself to the masses and so shows universalist features. It becomes an "out-group" and is liberal by inclination. The "sect" becomes an "association of those who are religiously qualified".

These sociologists consider that the Catholic religious orders belong to the "sect" type, but that they never in fact secede from the Catholic Church because of the overweening power of the centralized institution, through the intervention from outside. When we look at the history of religious life also in the period before Trent, it becomes clear that the religious within this Church are always "left" orientated, or, to use English political terminology, "Her Majesty's most loyal opposition." And when we look at the structures of religious life after Trent, we discover the paradoxical fact that religious life, the charismatic dimension within the Church, is most thoroughly institutionalized and therefore "right". This explains that the actual revision that is taking place in the great orders today is concerned with this institutionalization. On this point exemption might well be given a new theological meaning.[40] It could be a sign that religious life itself has enough community building energy to remain, with its own inspiration and its own kind of service, within the whole Church. It is a not negligible merit of Taizé that it does not identify itself with an existing ecclesiastical denomination and at the same time wants to avoid becoming a kind of elite Church. What is intended here is decentralization, not a structure imposed from on high by disciplinary obedience, but the formation of a community through like-mindedness, constantly animated by communal consultation.[41] The *Motu Proprio,* which gives some directives for the adaptation and renewal of religious life

[40] P. Huizing, "Exemptie van de religieuzen," in *Kath. Archief* 18, (April 26, 1963), pp. 418-29; W. Bertmans, "Die Exemption," in *Stimmen der Zeit* 86 (Aug., 1961), pp. 348-60.

[41] For Cuernavaca with its incorporation of psychoanalysis into the formation of the religious community, see *Doc. chr.* 1496 (June 18, 1967), col. 1150; (1965), col. 1885; (1966), col. 1811; G. Lemercier, *Dialogues avec le Christ. Moines en psycho-analyse* (Paris, 1966); *idem,* "Le monastère de Cuernavaca crée un centre psychoanalytique," in *Rev. Nouv.* 44 (1966), pp. 83-7.

after Vatican Council II, gently presses isolated communities with lack of vocations and with aged members to dissolve themselves or to link up with a similar-minded religious movement. One of the weakest spots of religious life is that there are too many religious institutions. This might be an argument for the manifold workings of the Spirit said to be active in the religious charism if there was not so much duplication in existing religious institutions, particularly in unintegrated reform movements. Rahner once pointed out that since Trent all religious reforms have come to form a kind of separate order. Does it not rather show that there is dispersion instead of communion when the new contribution of such a reform cannot be integrated within the same pattern of life? When Congar puts as the first and second conditions for a genuine reform of the Church the primacy of love and remaining within the community, this should hold first of all for the reform of religious institutions.

6. The De-Clericalization of Religious Life

Pursuing what we said above about a new understanding of exemption, we may say that history shows that the insertion of the religious into the functionary officialdom of the hierarchical Church did not encourage the development of a genuinely religious image of monastic institutions. This does not only apply to male religious. Female religious had a similar experience where they were completely incardinated into the official apostolate of the diocese.[42] This produced the curious phenomenon that in most institutions only priest-religious were accepted as full members, with an active and passive vote. On this point, renewal has already made great strides, particularly in those abbeys where the young candidates want to have a theological training but no longer wish to be ordained.[43] This has received juridical confirmation in that Vatican Council II has explicitly

[42] Cf. the numerous reactions to Cardinal Suenens' book *Kloosterleven en apostolaat* (Bruges/Utrecht, 1963).
[43] J. Daniélou, "La place des religieux dans la structure de l'Eglise," in *L'Eglise du Vatican II* (Paris, 1966), pp. 1173-80.

rejected a class distinction within the religious communities. It is obvious that this de-clericalization has been carried through in the secular institutes.[44]

Every overemphasis usually provokes an extreme reaction and so it is hardly astonishing that some[45] push this de-clericalization to the point where priesthood and religious life are said to be incompatible. This is a similar exaggerated contrast as that which is sometimes suggested between priesthood and prophetic function or between function and charism. The religious is prophetic precisely insofar as he opposes the turning of a means into an end. This end is often the religious institution itself, and so he will oppose that, too, in order that religious life may be the expression of what Christianity is meant to be.

7. Renewal and the Conciliar Documents of Vatican Council II

The first intention of Vatican Council II was to reach a new understanding of the Church by the Church itself. This obviously implied also a new understanding of religious life. At first it looked as if the drafters of the various schemata were going to repeat merely what the religious, and even more, Canon Law, had said about religious life since Trent. The first drafts of the decree on religious life presented it as a decree on the *vita regularis* (the regular life, life based on a rule) and disciplinary matters. The theology of religious life was to be taken up by the *Constitution on the Church.*[46] A positive indication that a genuine renewal was intended lay in the fact that the conciliar fathers were not satisfied with this juridical approach, except, strange to say, the religious themselves. From the first draft in 1962 till the definitive one in 1965 one can see that the conciliar debate took a more theological turn. The title, "the state of perfection to be achieved", was rejected; religious life is seen again as a dimension of the Church's life and concentrates on the imitation of Christ. The initial reference to the founder or foundress as the

[44] J. Beyer, "Les instituts séculiers," in Tillard, *op. cit.,* pp. 275-85.
[45] This is what Lemercier does where he explains his further plans about Cuernavaca; cf. *Inf. Cath. Int.* 291 (July 1, 1967), p. 12.
[46] A. Le Bourgeois, "Historique du décret," in Tillard, *op. cit.,* pp. 52-72.

source of renewal yields more and more to evangelical life as the fruitful starting point for bringing about renewal. The whole decree, however, shows marks of having been drafted in a hurry, as happened with other documents which were subject to the pressure of time at the end of the Council.

All this brought about that at first there was a certain disappointment with the decree. Perhaps the critical situation had led some to expect too much. The positive aspects of the Council's concern with religious life (Vatican I had not even mentioned it) does not lie so much in the concrete regulations as in the way it made room for an effective renewal. It appears that the word "reform" was deliberately avoided partly in order not to give the impression that religious life was declining, partly in order to bypass the loaded historical connotations of the word.

It is strange that the decree hardly pays any attention to religious life as it appears in other religions.[47]

Some have pointed out as an understandable yet regrettable defect in this decree that the text suffers from a certain ambiguity:[48] on the one hand it provides enough opportunity to "risk" certain steps forward (democratization, reform from below, experiments of smaller groups and the recognition of active religious life as of full value in its own right), but on the other, it offers those who, under pretext of loyalty to tradition, refuse to accept the need for reform, enough opportunities to block future progress. The overall impression one gathers from the abundant publications dealing with this decree is that naive admiration is yielding to a critical sense of renewal.[49] In general one may say that this renewal is proceeding faster among female religious than among their male counterpart. As the genuine religious pattern of life is becoming clearer the ethical demands

[47] S. P. de Roos, *De ethiek van de ongehuwde staat* (Nijkerk, 1964).

[48] F. Wulf, *op. cit.,* pp. 2-3.

[49] For a Protestant critical approach, see J. H. van Beusekom, *Het experiment der gemeenschap. Een onderzoek naare plaats en functie van de 'orde' in de reformatorische kerken* (The Hague, 1958); for the sociological aspect see H. Carrier and E. Pin, *Sociologie du Christianisme—Sociology of Christianity* (International Bibliography, Rome, 1964).

of religious life are necessarily stepped up and we should therefore expect a further decrease in the number of religious.[50]
Possibly there were too many religious anyway and the present
crisis may work as a catharsis.

8. Renewal and the Better Understanding of Theology and History

The future of religious life will be closely linked with the
future of theology. It will become increasingly impossible to look
on religious life as a monument that here and there needs a patch
of restoration which one could deal with by taking some disciplinary measures. The disciplinary element of religious life will
be determined by theology, particularly ecclesiology, not the
other way round. It is good to note that several General Chapters
since Vatican Council II began with such an ecclesiological re-
orientation.[51] Closely linked with this is a more acute understanding of the historicity of the Church. The next Concilium
volume on Church history will deal with this.[52]

This brief survey shows that the stirrings in religious life are
not a local phenomenon but one that appears throughout the
Church. Nor are they merely a list of complaints; on the contrary, the negative attitude that religious life would have no
future begins to yield to that of constructive criticism of a
reality at which religious life must aim and which is only partially
realized in its existing institutionalized form. Behind the institutionalization, clericalization and sacralization which have now
been overcome there is an intense search for new structures,
particularly by means of experiments undertaken by young religious groups so that there is hope for a renewed religious life.[53]

[50] For recent statistical data, see Pro mundi vita 18 (1967), "Vocations
des religieuses en Europe occidentale"; cf. 15, "Soeurs et frères autoch-
tones en Afrique."

[51] Cf. Paul VI's address to the General Chapter of the Franciscans, in
L'Osservatore Romano of June 24, 1967, p. 7.

[52] Concilium 34 (1968), on the prophetic element in Church history.

[53] J. G. Ranquet, Consécration baptismale et consécration religieuse
(Paris, ²1965); A. Fehringer, Dienst und Zeugnis. Die apostolische Sen-
dung der Ordensschwestern (Firedberg bei Augsburg, 1966), pp. 308-17.

In Memoriam:
John Courtney Murray, S.J.

John Courtney Murray, S.J., an associate editor of the Canon Law section of *Concilium,* died of a heart attack in New York on August 16. Father Murray was the ablest theologian to have appeared on the American Catholic scene. Most of his academic activity was taken up with teaching duties at Woodstock, Maryland, where for twenty-five years he also edited the esteemed *Theological Studies.* He was much sought after by non-Catholic institutions as lecturer, teacher and advisor. Twice he was a visiting professor of philosophy at Yale University. His talents included theoretical theology (the Trinity, grace), in which his *Problem of God* (Yale University Press, 1964) is a significant contribution to practical theology. It is in this latter field that he became internationally prominent, due to the role he played in the formation of the *Declaration on Religious Freedom* issued by Vatican Council II. He was present at the Council as an "expert" during the 2nd, 3rd and 4th sessions, and his sharp mind and firm thought is reflected in this document, which he himself described as substantially "in the line of the great American experiment—the First Amendment to the United States Constitution" (cf. his article "The Declaration on Religious Freedom" in *Concilium* 12 (1966), pp. 3-29). His book, *We Hold These Truths; Catholic Reflections on the American Proposition* (Sheed & Ward, 1960), is a thoughtful reflection upon the experience of the Catholic Church in the context of American life. His wit and sophistication are remembered in the reply which he gave to someone who asked if he were a liberal or a conservative; he described his position as being "in the extreme center".

In 1966 he was appointed director of the John La Farge Institute, which serves as a discussion center with American intellectuals concerning questions of a religious and sociological nature. Shortly before his death he had been serving as a consultant to a committee of the Episcopal Church concerning current theological problems, in particular the nature of heresy. In one of the last published statements he reflected upon the distinction between "adventurous answers which may well be mistaken" and "hardened positions which deserve to be called errors"—between a deficiency in intelligence and a deficiency in goodwill. John Courtney Murray was blessed with a striking intelligence and faithful goodwill. His loss will be felt not only in America but throughout the world. R.I.P.

BIOGRAPHICAL NOTES

LAMBERTO DE ECHEVERRÍA: Born in Vitoria, Spain, in 1918, he was ordained in 1941. He received doctorates in civil and canon law after studying at the universities of Salamanca and Madrid. He is a professor of the University of Salamanca, director of the Institute San Raymond de Peñafort, president of the editorial committee of *Revista Española de Derecho Canónico* and a member of the board of *Il Diritto ecclesiastico* (Rome). Among his published works are *El matrimonio en el Derecho canónico particular posterior al Código* (Vitoria, 1955) and *Función pastoral de los obispos* (Madrid, 1965). He is also the organizer in Salamanca of the "Semana de Derecho canónico".

TEODORO JIMÉNEZ-URRESTI: Born April 1, 1924, in Bilbao, Spain, he was ordained for that diocese in 1949. Studies at the Gregorian and the Lateran Universities in Rome led to a licentiate in dogmatic theology and a doctorate in canon law and Roman law. At present he is professor of dogmatic theology and Diocesan General Pro-Vicar. His published works include books in Spanish and numerous contributions to scholarly journals.

PETRUS HUIZING, S.J.: Born February 22, 1911, he became a Jesuit and was ordained in 1942. After studying at the University of Louvain, the Gregorian University in Rome and the University of Munich, he earned his doctorate in civil law in 1938 and in canon law in 1947. From 1946 to 1952 he was professor of canon law at the University of Maastricht, and from 1952 to 1964 at the Gregorian University in Rome.

✠ NEOPHYTOS EDELBY: Born November, 1920 in Alep, Syria, he pursued his studies at the Lateran University and at the Institutum Utriusque Iuris, both in Rome. He earned his doctorate "in utroque iure" in 1950. He was a professor in the Seminary of St. Anne in Jerusalem, then Secretary of the Holy Synod of the Greek-Melkite Church, and finally was consecrated titular archbishop of Edessa and appointed advisor to Patriarch Maximos IV. His published works include a book on the Byzantine missal and contributions to encyclopedias and reviews, especially *Proche-Orient Chrétien*.

PETER SHANNON: Born in Chicago in 1928, he was ordained in 1953. He studied at St. Mary's Seminary, Illinois, and at the Gregorian, Rome, receiving doctorates in theology and canon law. From 1965-66 he was president of the Canon Law Society of America, and now holds the posts of judge and lawyer to the Synod of the Archdiocese of Chicago. He is the author of "The Diriment Impediment of Mixed Religion (The Council of Trullo)," in *The Jurist* (July, 1963).

HANS HEIMERL: Born in Vienna in 1925, he was ordained in 1950. He studied at the University of Graz and at the Gregorian, Rome, received doctorates in theology in 1954 and in canon law in 1958, and qualified as lecturer in canon law in 1961. Since 1962 he has been professor of Church law at the University of Graz. Among his published works are *Laien im Dienste der Verkundigung: Laienmitwirkung an der Lehraufgabe der Kirche* (1958) and *Kirche, Klerus und Laien, Unterscheidungen und Beziehungen* (1965).

PAUL BOYLE, C.P.: Born in Detroit in 1932, he was ordained in 1953. He studied at the Angelicum and Lateran Colleges in Rome and at Evanston University, U.S.A. He holds degrees in theology and canon law, and since 1957 has lectured in these subjects at St Meinrad's Seminary, Indiana, U.S.A. He is executive secretary of the Canon Law Society of America and is also president of this society's Central Committee of Coordination. He is the author of "The Diocesan Curia and Religious Women," in *Attitudes and Structures* (Davenport, Iowa, 1966).

HUBERT PROESMANS, C.S.S.R.: Born in Belgium in 1912, he was ordained in the Redemptorist Order in 1936. He studied at the Angelicum in Rome and at Louvain University, gaining his doctorate in theology in 1948. Since 1940 he has been professor of moral theology at the house of the Redemptorist Fathers in Louvain, where he has been superior since 1965. Among his works is "De theologie van de religieuze roeping," in De Kloosterling (1964).

CHARLES MUNIER: Born in France in 1922, he was ordained in 1948. He studied at the Canon Law Institute and Theological School at Strasbourg, and the Vatican School of Paleography, receiving doctorates in canon law, literature and theology. He has been dean of studies of the Canon Law Institute at Strasbourg since 1958 and assistant lecturer at the School of Catholic Theology at Strasbourg University. His published works include "Concilia Galliae a.314-506," in *Corpus Christianorum* (1963), and "Droit canonique et Droit romain d'après Gratien et les Décrétistes," in *Melanges Le Bras* (1964). He is a frequent contributor to the Strasbourg journal *Revue des Sciences religieuses*.

JOHN OESTERREICHER: Born in Austria in 1904, he was ordained in 1927. He studied at the School of Medicine in the University of Vienna and at the theology schools of the Universities of Vienna and Graz. He is a doctor of theology and is director of the Institute of Jewish-Christian Studies at Seton Hall University, Newark, U.S.A. His published works include *The Israel of God* (Englewood Cliffs, 1963).

IVAN ŽUŽEK, S.J.: Born September 2, 1924, in Ljubljana, Yugoslavia, he became a Jesuit and was ordained in 1955. He pursued his studies at the

Pontifical Oriental Institute, and he earned a licentiate in canon law at the Gregorian University in Rome. He has been professor of Oriental canon law at the Oriental Institute since 1963. His published works include *Studies on the Chief Code of Russian Canon Law* and contributions to *Orientalia Christiana Periodica*.

International Publishers of CONCILIUM

ENGLISH EDITION
Paulist Press
Glen Rock, N. J., U.S.A.

Burns & Oates Ltd.
25 Ashley Place
London, S.W.1

DUTCH EDITION
Uitgeverij Paul Brand, N. V.
Hilversum, Netherlands

FRENCH EDITION
Maison Mame
Tours/Paris, France

JAPANESE EDITION (PARTIAL)
Nansôsha
Tokyo, Japan

GERMAN EDITION
Verlagsanstalt Benziger & Co., A.G.
Einsiedeln, Switzerland

Matthias Grunewald-Verlag
Mainz, W. Germany

SPANISH EDITION
Ediciones Guadarrama
Madrid, Spain

PORTUGUESE EDITION
Livraria Morais Editora, Ltda.
Lisbon, Portugal

ITALIAN EDITION
Editrice Queriniana
Brescia, Italy